First the
FIRE,
Then the
LIE

ELAINE NELSON

PAGE PUBLISHING, INC.
Conneaut Lake, PA

First originally published by Page Publishing 2021

ISBN 978-1-6624-4815-7 (pbk)
ISBN 978-1-6624-4816-4 (digital)

Printed in the United States of America

My first dedication is to my God and Creator, who gave me joy, peace, and a sound mind and then empowered me to write this book.

My second dedication goes to my grandmother Ruth Hall. She taught me the meaning of love by her example of loving me.

My third dedication goes to all the foster children still in the system or group homes, to all the children who have aged out of the foster care system and now have become adults trying to find their way, and to all the foster parents and social workers who work so hard in loving and sacrificing their time to make a difference in a child's life.

My fourth dedication goes to three individuals—Minister T. D. Jakes, Oprah Winfrey, and Tyler Perry. Thank you for helping me to find my voice by way of listening to yours.

ACKNOWLEDGMENTS

· · · · · · · · · · · ·

First, I would like to thank my children—my intelligent and handsome son, John Nelson, and my brilliant and beautiful daughter, Angelique Nelson; my loving grandson, Cameron Gregory, an engineer graduate; and my beautiful granddaughter, Carman Gregory, a singer, dancer, and registered nurse.

Thanks to all the teams' players who worked so hard and contribute their time and support: the platinum team—Joyce Arterberry of Alabama, Katrina Parker of Illinois, Sheryl Rogers of Missouri, Mr. Jerry Lucky of Alabama, Sumayyah Amatullah of Georgia, Diana Davis of California, and Kenneth Vines of Colorado; the gold team—James Griffin of Alabama, J. D. McBride of Missouri, Savannah Gumphrey of Alabama, DeAngelo Meeks of Alabama, Lynn Goldstein of Missouri, Monica Vaughn of Colorado, and Mary Ann Harris of Illinois; and the silver team—Alexander Wiegand of Alabama, Monica Adams of Missouri, James Sanchez of Alabama, Eddie Williams of Alabama, Jourdan Ways, and Mr. Clay of Alabama.

A special thanks to Chuck Shank of Page Publishing for hanging in there with me and Lana Beers also of Page Publishing for showing such kindness and patience.

I would like to thank everyone from bottom of my heart.

CHAPTER 1

. . . .

It began with me and my doll Amy sitting on the front steps of our housing projects. I was only five years old at the time. Amy and I were enjoying watching the children in the neighborhood play. I heard my mom's and sisters' voices from inside the house. They were sitting around laughing and talking, while my mom was in the kitchen cooking. My doll Amy and I often sat on the front steps of our apartment because I enjoyed looking at the big mountain that sat right in front of our apartment. It looked like it was in walking distance because it was so big; but it was not. It was actually many miles away. My mom told me it had a name called Pikes Peak. I never knew why, but I always loved looking at the mountains. So I shared the mountain view with my doll, Amy.

After sitting on the stairs for a period, I decided to go into the house and join my family. Once I opened the door and entered, I could see my sisters to the right. There was Lena the oldest sister, Oma next to the oldest, Lorraine, Rosie, and me. I was the youngest. We were all about a year apart in birth dates. They were just sitting around talking girl talk. My mom was in the kitchen preparing lunch. She was whistling and singing, as she frequently did. She had a beautiful voice and whistled like a bird. Not only did she have a beautiful voice but she was also beautiful. She was tall with wavy black hair flowing down her back. Oma, who we affectionately called Ommie, and Lorraine had hair like my mom's. They could all style and brush their hair by just using a brush, oil, and water. Mom's complexion was light brown, like Ommie and Lorraine. Unlike Lena, Rosie, and me, all had darker complexions, and our hair was coarse in texture.

Our hair was not as long either. It barely came to our shoulders. We had to get our hair pressed with the hot comb, and I did not like that one bit (but that was the way it was).

I walked straight inside the front door. There were about twelve gray concrete steps leading the way to the upstairs floor. I really needed to go upstairs and get a brush to brush my baby doll's hair, but I did not feel like climbing those stairs. They were a bit much for a five-year-old to climb. Plus, I had already fallen down a couple times and hit my head on the concrete! So I decided to just go inside the front room with my sisters and enjoy listening to them talk. As I got comfortable listening to my sisters and watching my mother cook in the kitchen, I began to fall asleep. Then all of a sudden, I heard a big bang, a big and loud banging. Somebody was kicking the door. *Bam*, it sounded like some man shouting and swearing. Suddenly, I recognized the voice. It was my mother's old boyfriend, Limo. He was yelling and cursing and calling out my mother's name. He was saying he was going to kill her. He was yelling in a mean, angry voice, saying what he planned to do to her once he got his hands on her. He continued to beat on the door. My mom dropped what she was doing in the kitchen. She ran and grabbed me so fast by my little arm, squeezing my arm ever so tightly and pulling me as she was pushing my sisters up the stairs. When we reached the top of the stairs, I turned and looked back at the door. I could see the door vibrating from the beating that was being put on it. That was when my little legs speeded up. The bathroom was straight ahead at the top of the stairs. On the right was my mother's bedroom.

My mom pushed us all into her room, then she pushed me down under her bed and told me to stay there. Then she pushed my sisters Rosie, Lorraine, and Ommie onto the floor on the other side of the bed. She told them also to get under the bed and not move. She pulled Lena toward the entrance of the bedroom, where the closet was located. She grabbed Lena by her shoulders and looked her in the eye and spoke, "If anything happens to me, take care of your sisters," then she pushed Lena in the closet. She turned again to me and my sisters. "If anything happens to me, girls, I mean anything, I love you and do not ever forget it. I will always love you no matter what happens." Then she turned and ran to the bathroom. The loud banging was still going on downstairs. As she ran into the bathroom, slamming the bathroom door behind her, she left the bedroom door open where we were hiding, so we had a clear view of the bathroom. As the bathroom door slammed, I could hear the front door being torn off the hinges. I could hear the door collapse when it hit the floor. *Bam, bam,* it was a loud, horrible sound. The door had finally collapsed under the pressure of the beating he had put on it.

I could hear his feet running up the stairs and his voice getting closer and closer as he continued cursing and yelling my mother's name. I was shaking; my little heart was about to beat out of my little chest. Ommie was crying, and I could see Lorraine trying to cover her mouth. She was whispering to Ommie, saying, "If you do not shut up, he is going to hear you and find us." Lena was standing at the entrance of the door. It looked like she had something in her hand. She had a terrified and a bold, unafraid look on her face all at the same time. It was as if she was saying to herself, "No one is getting past this door." Then Limo reached the top of the stairs and went straight to the bathroom door, as if he knew exactly where my mother was hiding. He started beating and kicking on the door. I could see his back even though I was under the bed. He began slamming his upper body against the door and continued kicking it, making all kinds of loud sounds, *boom* and *bam*. My mom was not saying anything at that time. I was sure she was hoping the door held up and he went away. But instead, he burst open into the bathroom. I heard my mother scream for the first time in my life. It was horrible.

I wanted to help her. I felt so helpless. She started screaming words like "Oh no! Jesus, please help me. Do not let him kill me!" She started begging for her life, begging him to please stop. She cried out as he continued to punch, kick, and choke her. She said, "You are going to kill me if you do not stop." As she continued to scream, he lunged on her. I could see his fist go up and come down repeatedly, hitting her. I could hear his fist hitting her body. It sounded like a boxer in a boxing ring when he hit his opponent. It was the most horrible sound that I had ever heard. My mom hollered out every time he hit her. Eventually, he knocked her into the bathtub. That was when the sounds changed. The sounds were more like a loud thumping and pounding sound. It must have been part of her head or skull hitting the sides of the tub or the walls in the bathroom. He continued until her voice became silent. There were no more sounds coming from my mom.

Just as she became silent, you could hear the sirens in the background. They were police or ambulance sirens. They seemed to be getting closer and closer. Evidently, Limo also heard the sirens while he was cursing and yelling repeatedly, "I hope you die." After the approaching sirens got nearer, I heard him saying, "I got to get the hell out of here." Then he emerged from the bathroom door like a big, tall monster. I shrunk further under the bed, trying to be still and silent. I could see his feet as he walked away from the bathroom and toward the bedroom. When he turned toward the hall light, I saw the front of him, and he was covered in blood. Blood was all over him. Blood covered his hands and clothes, and there was even blood on his face. He took a step toward our room. I thought we must be next. Then the sirens sounded like they were at our front door. That was when he turned from walking toward our room and began running down the stairs. I could hear the loud sirens and the car wheels screeching as the police vehicles were trying to come to a complete stop. At the same time, I could hear the backdoor slam as Limo ran out of the house. That was when I jumped out from under the bed and ran in the bathroom to see how bad my mom was hurt. I was wondering if she was still alive. She was lying in the bathtub covered in blood. There was blood everywhere. I tried to wake her up, but she was unconscious. I began to shake her as I was yelling, "Wake up, Mommy, wake up!" I started crying uncontrollably and screamed repeatedly, "Wake up, Mommy, wake up, Mommy, please!" I was trying to lift her head, but it was too heavy.

Then the paramedics came rushing through the door and ran up the stairs. Next thing I knew, the paramedics were trying to pull me off my mother. I was crying, holding on to my mother and telling the paramedics to let me go as they tried to lift me off my mother. I kept yelling I did not want to go. The paramedics asked my sister Lena, who was standing at the door, to "please get your little sister."

Once Lena pulled me off my mother, we were instructed to go downstairs and have a seat so they could tend to my mother's wounds. While sitting downstairs on the couch, I watched the paramedics run up and down the stairs, carrying all types of medical supplies. Then it seemed as if my grandparents appeared out of nowhere. My grandmother ran through the door straight toward me and my sisters. My grandfather ran straight up the stairs to my mom. My grandmother was frantically yelling with tears in her eyes. Her arms stretched out, trying to hug us all at the same time. She was trying to yell, although she was almost out of breath, asking repeatedly, "Girls, are you all right? Did he hurt any of you?"

We all replied, "No, but Momma is upstairs hurt bad. Please go help her."

Gran turned and ran up the stairs. As she was running up the stairs, she looked back and said, "Girls, everything is going to be okay. Just sit tight. Stay right there."

Meanwhile, my grandfather had come back downstairs. He was at the front entrance, trying to assist the police officer in removing the front door off the floor and propping it against the wall. They needed to make a clear path. Just as they were removing the door off the floor, more paramedics came in with a long stretcher. They were preparing my mom to be secured for the move and brought downstairs. The ambulance backed up into our yard almost to our front door. As I was sitting there in the front room, I glanced out the window. I saw so many people from our neighborhood in our yard. They were all trying to look inside our house. They were standing in our front yard. Some of them were trying to peep in the front windows. A couple of them were trying to peep inside the front door. They were all trying to see what was going on because we had so many police in our home. I felt so hurt and helpless. After my grandmother had been upstairs helping the paramedics, she walked down the stairs in front of them, making sure the path was clear. There were two men in the front and two on each side of the stretcher. I watched intently as they were bringing her down the stairs. I was listening for her to say something, moan, or groan, anything; but she was silent and motionless. There was no crying or making one single sound. I was hoping she would give me a wave or something. I came to the conclusion that she was still unconscious as they loaded her into the ambulance.

My grandmother told us to go get in the station wagon. My grandparents owned a tan and brown Rambler station wagon. It had three rows of seats and a long, flat area in the back that you could lie down on. While we were waiting in the car, my grandmother did her best to clean up all the blood that was in the bathroom. She also made sure to clean the kitchen and make sure the stove was turned off where my mom had been cooking. As we continued to wait in the car, I saw my grandfather and a police working hard to secure the front door. They were trying to make sure no other intruders could break in. They were hammering some nails and pieces of broken wood from the door in order to secure it. My sisters and I continued to sit in the car, patiently waiting on our grandparents. My sister Ommie was still whimpering and crying a little bit, while the rest of us were just sitting and being silent. When my grandparents finished securing the house, they got in the car, and we were all on our way to their house.

CHAPTER 2

. . . .

Wisdom, Joy, and Pain

My grandparents told us we would be living with them for a while at least until my mother's health was good enough for her to care for us again. My grandmother said when our mom got out of the hospital, we would be moving to some different projects located not too far from their house. This would make it easier for them to assist my mother. The ride to my grandparents' house seemed like it took forever. I had ridden there before, but this time, it seemed so far away. My grandparents lived in a small town called Globeville, Colorado. It was located right outside of the North Central city limits of Denver. When we got about one mile from my grandmother's house, my grandmother called out in a loud voice "Oh, girls, look, this is where your new home is going to be."

I raised my head up from drifting off to sleep and saw what looked like a school, a big redbrick building about three stories tall. I asked my grandmother, "What kind of building is that?" as I pointed to the building.

She replied, "No, Laney, not that building. You are pointing at the building for disabled children."

I asked, "What are disabled children?" Then I saw a little boy in front of the building getting out of a bus. He was dragging one foot and twisting his body on crutches, struggling to enter the facility where he must have lived.

My grandmother continued to explain, "Some children are less fortunate than you and your sisters. For example, that young man you are looking at appears to have a disability. He is struggling to make his way into the building. His disability is no fault of his own. He was born that way."

I felt something at that moment inside me. Even though I was just a child, I began to have compassion and empathy for that young man, seeing him struggle with things that I took for granted. From that moment, I stopped thinking about myself and all the bad stuff that had just happened to my mother just a few hours ago. I started thinking how blessed my mom was to have had a normal life. She had given birth to children that did not have any disabilities. At that time, a peace came over me that I could not explain. I wanted to tell my grandmother, but I did not have the words in my vocabulary nor did I understand, at five years old, why I was having these thoughts and feelings. Then I heard my grandmother say "Laney" in a loud voice. That was the nickname my grandmother and family called me. Then Gran, short for Grandmother, said, "Laney, are you listening to me? I said your new home is going to be in one of these project buildings, not in the redbrick building called Larden Hall for handicapped children. Do you understand what I am saying?"

I replied, "Yes, Gran, I understand."

There were a lot of projects in that housing complex. It looked like about twenty different buildings. They were similar to the projects that we had just left. They just looked to be a little newer. As we got to the end of the project complex, the road changed from a paved black city road to an unpaved brown dirt road. We were leaving the city limits of Denver and entering the town of Globeville. As we continued down the dirt road, about three blocks on the left-hand side set a little white church with a steeple on top. It looked like one of those little churches out of a storybook. My grandmother excitedly said, "Look, girls, there is my church on the left." She continued speaking in a loud, excited voice, "I am now the mother of that church. And now you all will be able to go to church with me and sit beside me during service. I know I will have to buy you girls some church clothes, but I will work it out."

Further down the road, there were a few houses scattered a good distance from one another. Then we came up on three homes on the right sitting side by side. My grandmother said, "There is our house, girls, the one in the center. They are really all ours because we own all three, but we rent out the other two. We bought them with some of the Indian money we got." We did not know what she was talking about Indian money, and we really did not care. We just replied, "Okay, Gran," and she continued talking about how nice her neighbors were. And on the left, I saw a girl and a boy, children that looked to be around my age playing in the yard. As my grandfather was parking the station wagon, I looked out the window and saw chickens running around in my grandmother's yard. I ask my granny if the chickens would bite me. Everybody in the car started laughing. They seemed to get a good laugh out of my question. My grandmother replied, "No, Laney, they do not bite."

We began unloading our belongings and heading into my grandparents' home. It was a one-story redbrick home with a small front porch, and it had two bedrooms, one bath, a kitchen, a large front room, and a big backyard. As we entered the house, the first thing I noticed was a square brown cabinet with a round glass in the front of it placedon the floor. I asked my grandmother, "What is that?"

She replied, "That is called a TV, and over in the other corner is a radio. These are not toys. They cost a lot of money, and they are not to be played with."

I asked her what they did.

She replied, "They are for entertainment and getting information. You will get a chance to watch TV and listen to the radio on Saturdays and Sunday evenings."

As I was continuing to admire her house, my uncle came into the room. He grabbed me, picked me up, and swung me around. At the same time he was swinging me around, he was asking me, "Do you remember your uncle Arvet?

I replied, "I think so." I only said that because I wanted him to hurry up and put me down. He was kind of scary to me. His eyes were crossed and moving in all directions. Later that day, I asked my grandmother why my uncle Arvet's eyes moved so fast from left to right.

She explained, "When he was born, the doctor put the wrong eyedrops in his eye during the time of delivery. And those drops that were put in his eyes caused him to be partially blind in both eyes." Then she said, "That is why he has always lived with me after all of the rest of my children married and moved away. I have been helping your uncle all of his life." That answered a lot of my questions about Uncle Arvet. That helped me to better understand his condition and not be afraid of him anymore. At the end of the day, my grandmother called me and my sisters to come join her in the front room. She said she wanted to make sure we understood that the change in our living situation was not our fault. She continued to say, "I want you girls to be confident and proud of yourselves and never let anyone tell you that you are less than another person. No matter what color your skin is or texture of your hair, God made us all equal." I believed her about the color of my skin, but I still had a problem with my hair being equal to my sisters because they did not have to get their hair pressed, with the hot comb. Then she said, "There are going to be times that I will not be there to help or protect you. But God will always be there no matter what the situation is." That was why I liked my grandmother so much. She had a way with words that made me feel at peace even in a teaching moment.

After her talk on life's lessons, Gran said it's time for us to go to bed. My sisters all slept together on one big pallet on the front-room floor. Since I was the baby, I got a chance to sleep in the bed with my grandmother. My grandmother informed us that our grandfather no longer spent nights at their house, but he would be back in the morning for breakfast. I did not ask any questions as I figured as long as he was coming back in the morning, they must be okay. Plus, that meant I got a chance to sleep with Granny, another name for Gran. She had a big bed that smelled of Bengay and Vicks VapoRub. Those were her two favorite remedies. Oh, and do not let me forget about another one of her favorite remedies called Glover's mane. She loved to put that stinky ointment on my head, trying to make my hair grow. But that night, no Glover's mane, just me and my Granny snuggled under one blanket and one of Granny's homemade quilts. As I was about to fall asleep, I saw my grandmother get down on her knees on the side of the bed. She folded her hands and began to pray. I never saw my mother pray, so it was fascinating to watch and listen to my grandmother's prayers. She spoke like she was talking to someone right there, as if someone was really listening to her every word. She was saying things like "Please protect my children and her children's children." I remembered that prayer because it included me. I did not know this God or Jesus that she spoke of. I just liked listening to her pray until I would fall asleep.

After a few days had passed, it was Sunday. It was time to go to church. If you were lucky enough to spend a Saturday night at my grandmother's house, you were going to church on Sunday morning. That was just the way it was, no questions asked. Everybody knew you were going; it was not up for debate. I did not mind going to church at all. I just could not understand what the preacher was saying. He always sounded like he had a breathing problem, he could not catch his breath, or he needed to cough something out of his throat. I just figured I was a child and not supposed to understand. The more I went, the more I liked going. When getting ready for church on Sunday mornings, Gran would brush my hair and put ribbons on all my little braids. She would make some of our clothes and undergarments. Gran made us petticoats and half-slips. These were undergarments that we wore under our dresses. The purpose of the slip was to keep people from seeing through your skirt or dress, and the purpose of the petticoat was to make your skirt flare out; it was the style. The problem was, my grandmother made the petticoat out of a material that was called gunnysacks. Gunnysacks got their name from sacks that were used for carrying potatoes. The petticoats would itch and scratch me so bad, but I did not complain because my grandmother would brag on how much time she spent making her granddaughters' petticoats and how she saved so much money using gunnysack material. She would also starch and iron my little white dress with pink ruffles until it would be wrinkle free and crisp like a new summer day. When I put on my dress and my black patent leather shoes, I felt like I was someone special.

After church, later that evening, Gran gathered me and my sisters around the TV. She said she wanted us to watch the five o'clock news with her. And after the news, we could watch a couple of her favorite shows. *The Lawrence Welk Show*, *The Ed Sullivan Show*, and the Billy Graham church broadcast were a few of her favorites. I was so excited. I had never seen a TV show before. Then the news came on, and they were talking about people protesting in the South. As the news continued, it was horrible and hard to watch. There were colored people getting beaten in the streets like dogs. I even saw a police dog biting a man. It was crazy. My grandmother said, "I know the news was hard for you to look at, but I wanted you girls to see and be aware of what is going on in the world." She continued to say, "Just because this does not happen here in our town does not mean it is not in other towns. Some people must deal with this every day in the Southern states. That is why those people you saw on TV were marching for their equal rights, like we have here in Denver. So do not ever take for granted your freedom because people have fought and died for your freedom. Then she said, "I do not ever want you to forget what you just saw. Do you understand me?"

We all replied, "Yes, Gran, we understand."

Then she said, "Promise me one thing, that you will not go to the South."

We all shook our heads and agreed with her.

"There is one more thing I must share with you."

I said to myself, "Oh, my goodness, what else could it be?"

She began talking about how her great grandfather was an Indian chief, and she was born on a reservation. When she was thirteen years old, her great grandfather made a trade with some white man. The white men had blankets that they wanted to trade in exchange for some animal furs. The problem was that the white men's blankets were infected with the smallpox disease. She went on to say that she contracted smallpox from the blankets along with several other members of her tribe. She told us how they had to isolate her along with the other infected members of her tribe. She said they built small wooden house for the infected called death houses. Gran said she was placed in one of the houses to die. They would bring her food and water and leave it at her door because it was highly contagious and there was no vaccine. She said, as she approached her last days, a man came and prayed that she would be healed, and she was healed instantly. She said they had to get a doctor's approval before she could leave the death house. Then Gran said in a loud voice, "Girls, look at me. You see I am still alive due to a miracle. That means you are alive due to a miracle because you came from me. That is why I wanted to share this story with you. So you should never give up no matter how bad it is or what it looks like." She then gave us all a big, long hug, as if she were putting power in each of us with a hug. I did not understand a lot at the time, but those stories stuck with me as the days went on. I thought about them repeatedly.

After a couple more weeks went by, my aunt Dorothy came over. She wanted to inform my grandmother that she and her husband, Uncle Eddie, had decided that they wanted to keep me and my sisters for a few weeks to give my grandmother a break. Gran was truly thankful and gladly accepted their offer. Aunt Dorothy and Uncle Eddie had a two-story redbrick house. It had four bedrooms and one bathroom. There was a long wooden staircase that led upstairs, where all the bedrooms were located. We stayed with them for a couple of weeks. I must say, it was not bad at all even though we six slept on one bed. We were treated the same as the rest of the family. I had a lot of fun playing with my cousins. I was closest to my cousins Paul, Bobo, and Connie because we were all around the same age. They had another brother named Eddie and two more sisters named Runince and Vicky. They all seemed eager to share their home with us. Aunt Dorothy was a good cook, and Uncle Eddie did his best to help keep things running smoothly around the house.

After a couple weeks with no problems, our stay had come to an end, and our grandparents returned to pick us back up, just like they said they would. We gathered our things and said our goodbyes. We got back into our grandparents' station wagon, and we were on our way back to our grandparents' house. While riding in the car, our grandmother said she had good news. She had been informed that our mother would be getting out of the hospital on the upcoming weekend. It was going to be the Thanksgiving holiday weekend. Gran went on to say that my mom's doctor recommended she should spend this time with her children. Their hope was that this would help to stimulate her healing process. My grandmother said we should not expect too much from her at first. She still had a long road ahead to recovery. Finally, we arrived back to my grandmother's house. I saw Becky and John playing in their yard next door. I could barely wait to get out of the car so I could tell them all about my stay with my cousins and give them the good news about my mom coming home for Thanksgiving. I was super excited because that meant all my aunts, uncles, and cousins that lived out of town would be there. Thanksgiving was a time when it was mandatory to be at my grandmother's house.

On the week before Thanksgiving, my grandmother would give me and my sisters kitchen chores. After an exhausting week watching and trying to help my grandmother and sisters with the preparations for Thanksgiving dinner, it was finally the day before Thanksgiving. That night, I slept peacefully and woke to the sound of several voices of my relatives in the front room. Then I heard someone say my mother's name. I jumped out of bed and ran to the front room. My grandmother was standing in the front room. She told me my mom was sitting at the kitchen table, and she was waiting on us to go talk to her one at a time. My grandmother did not want us to overwhelm my mother by speaking all at once. I wanted to run past my grandmother and go give my mom a big hug, but my grandmother said, "Hold on, Lane, you got to wait your turn. Remember what I told you, she still has a long road to recovery." So I went and washed up and brushed my teeth and got dressed. Then I took a seat in the front room and waited for my turn. My aunts and uncles were also waiting for a chance to speak with my mom as one person went in the kitchen another person came out. My sisters and I were the last to go in.

Then finally, it was my turn. I noticed as I walked toward the kitchen that none of my sisters were smiling as they left the kitchen. Once it was my turn, I rushed into the kitchen with my arms wide open and with a big smile, saying, "Hi, Mommy, are you okay? It is me, Laney." I said it in a loud voice. I was looking at her straight in her eyes, and she looked right past me, like she could not see me. Then I said to her again, "Mommy, it is me, Laney. You know, Big Head." That was the nickname she gave me. I said, "I missed you so much I wanted to help you, but I could not do anything." Then I looked at her again and asked her if she could hear me. Then I laid my head down on her knees and put her hands on top of my head and slid her hands back and forth over my head. She used to say she loved rubbing my head. Then I took her hand and slowly moved it over my face, hoping this would help her to recognize me, but I got no response. Suddenly, she turned her head and looked at me. As she turned, she tried to smile, but she could not because her mouth was wired shut. I could see the wires in her mouth, and seeing her like that broke my heart. I became so sad I could not speak. The wires in her mouth brought back all the bad memories from that horrible day she was beaten. I could not say anything else. I just got up and leaned over and gave her a big hug and kissed her on her cheek and walked away. I did not go back and try to talk to her again. I could not stand seeing her in that condition. I knew right then it was going to be a long time before we would be able to go back home with our mother. So I said to myself I might just as well get used to spending more weekdays with the neighbors' children.

I tried hanging around my grandmother as much as possible, but she was a busy woman. I looked forward to the end of the day right before bedtime because that was when I got a chance to sit at my grandmother's feet and listen to her read powerful Bible stories. I did not know or understand the significance of listening to all those Bible stories at that time. I just liked the way they sounded when she read them and the way she rubbed my head until I would fall asleep. The next morning, we all had our chores to do. My job was collecting the eggs out of the henhouse. It did not matter how young you were. If you lived at my grandmother's house, you helped by doing some kind of work. My grandmother always said, "If you can walk, talk, and eat, there was a job you could do." She had a chicken coop where the rooster hung out and the chickens laid their eggs. Gran taught me how to carry and hold the egg baskets and place the eggs in the baskets without breaking them or disturbing the chickens in their nests. I asked my grandmother if I could have one of the baby chickens. She said no, but she would try to get me a pet to play with. About a week or two later, she came home with a box. She said she had a little surprise for me. She handed me the box, and I could hear something moving inside. I opened the box, and it was a beautiful baby rabbit. It was white all over, had a pink nose, and had a round and fluffy tail. It was small enough to fit in the palm of my hands. Gran must have known I was having a hard time trying to adjust to the absence of my mother, so she got me my very own pet. I pulled the rabbit up by the chest and hugged it so tight. Then I named my rabbit Pinky because of its bright-pink nose.

Over the course of a few months, I had begun to adapt to my new environment and my grandmother's house along with my sisters. My rabbit, Pinky, was growing so fast. I asked my granny if she could please get Pinky a bigger cage to sleep in. Meanwhile, the neighbors who lived next door on the right, Mr. and Mrs. Fox, did not have any children of their own, and Mr. Fox was constantly trying to start up a conversation with me. He would ask me questions about myself and my rabbit all the time. And for some reason, he was showing a lot of interest in Pinky. I did not think much of it at the time. I just figured he liked kids and rabbits. Until one morning, I woke up and went outside to feed Pinky, and there was no Pinky anywhere. I ran and told my grandmother that Pinky was not in her cage. Gran told me not to worry. Pinky would show up when she got hungry. I saw my neighbor Mr. Fox in his backyard, and I went immediately up to him to inquire if he had seen Pinky. As I approached the fence, I yelled out, "Mr. Fox, have you seen my rabbit, Pinky?"

He replied, "Who? What did you say?"

"You know, Pinky, my rabbit, have you seen her?"

He replied, "Sorry, but we ate that rabbit."

I asked, "What do you mean?" as my heart sunk to my feet.

He replied, "Just like I said, we ate the rabbit. Your rabbit came over in our yard, and we ate it."

I could not believe what I was hearing. My mind was trying to understand what he was saying while I was getting sick to my stomach. I wanted to hit and kick him so bad, but I just went into the house and told my grandmother what he said. My grandmother was highly upset, like I had never seen her before. She told me to wait in the house while she went over to Mr. and Mrs. Fox's house to have a talk with them. When she returned, she said she was so sorry for what happened to Pinky, but I did not have to worry about Mr. and Mrs. Fox anymore. They would be moving in a couple of weeks. It was not long after that that they were gone.

After several more months had come and gone, my grandmother informed us that our mother was getting out of the hospital soon, and we would be moving into our new project. My grandmother said she was fortunate to have found my mother a three-bedroom apartment so fast, and she was already approved. Gran instructed us to start informing our friends in the neighborhood that we would be moving soon. Although I loved my grandmother, I was eager to get back home with my mom. On the day my mom was released from the hospital, my grandparents took her straight to her apartment. Gran and Papa were right there trying their best to help my mom get her house set up before my sisters and I could move in. After about a week of preparation, our new apartment was ready for us to join our mother. At the end of the following week, we loaded up the station wagon, and we were on our way to join Mom at our new home.

CHAPTER 3

. . . .

Mom Gets Out of the Hospital

At first, when my mom got home, she slept a lot. I did not think much of it at first until I saw she was not interested in much of anything. When she did utter a word or two, it was to designate most of the household responsibilities to my sister Lorraine. Lorraine's nickname was Raney. Each month, my mother would give Raney a portion of the welfare check that she received monthly. Raney was supposed to buy groceries for our entire family, which was supposed to last a month. Instead, Raney would come back from the store with hot dogs, potato chips, soda, ice cream, and Twinkies. This food would last about three days.

I became friends with the little Hispanic girl who lived next door named Edna. She was my age and the only child in her family. Edna and I became good friends instantly. I asked her to join me for a food party that I would have at the first of each month when Raney bought the food. We would take all our food upstairs in my bedroom and sit in front of the window and eat and laugh. The first time we met, we were both playing in front of our yards. She was trying to talk to me, but I could not understand her because she did not speak English and I did not speak Spanish, so we decided to teach each other. At the beginning of each month, Edna and I feasted like queens for a few days. After that, the food from the welfare check ran out. I was back to eating whatever I could find, and Edna did not come back until the first of the next month. In between welfare checks, I was starving. I had to resort to searching for food anywhere I could find it. I found the quickest and easiest way to get food was right outside my back door in the neighbor's trash cans. Each tenant had their very own trash can that was metal and silver in color in their backyard. Sometimes I would have to confront a dog or two, but that did not bother me because I felt like all dogs liked me and we understood one another, so I was not afraid of them. To make them move away from the trash cans, I would simply say, "You had your turn, and now it is my turn, so go away." Most of the time, that worked.

After a while, I realized the dogs were beating me to all the good stuff by getting to the trash early in the morning. So I started getting out earlier in the mornings. Then I found myself in situations having to deal with more aggressive dogs. These dogs were not responding to my voice. I had to throw rocks at these dogs to get them to move. It was just getting too dangerous fighting off dogs just to get a decent meal every day. Then I saw a big truck picking up a huge dumpster. The truck had two long metal prongs on each side of it that were used to lift the dumpster and take it away. Right then I got a bright idea! I said to myself, "I bet there is a lot of good stuff in that dumpster." So I went through the project complex searching for more dumpsters like that one, hoping that they had not been emptied yet. I found about six dumpsters. I could not believe that I had not noticed the big dumpsters before now. As I was walking and searching, I found one dumpster that the truck driver had not emptied for whatever reason. "It must be my lucky day!" I shouted. Now I only had to find a way to reach the side opening. The opening was so high. It was above my head. I definitely had to find something to stand on to reach the opening. The dumpsters had sliding metal doors on each side of it.

Because I was too short to reach the opening on my own, I looked around the neighborhood until I found a big box. I propped the box in front of the opening, then I climbed on top of the box, and it was a perfect fit. I was now able to access the opening. I took one look in that dumpster and saw not only food, but I also saw clothes and toys. My eyes lit up like it was Christmas Day. I dove right into the dumpster headfirst. The first thing I found was a child's coat. I hurried up and tried it on. It was gray and had big white buttons going down the front. It was a little big, but I liked it anyway. Then I saw some toys and a half-eaten burrito. I snuggled up in the coat and sat right there in the dumpster and enjoyed my burrito as I played with my newly found toys. As I was playing with the toys, I got sleepy, and I covered myself with the trash like a blanket and fell asleep. Right there in the dumpster was where I got one of the best nights' sleep in a long while.

When the sun aRosie the next morning, the first thing I thought about was I was going to get in trouble for not coming home all night, but hopefully I would be able to explain how I just fell asleep. I hurried up and hopped out the dumpster and ran home. When I walked in the door, my mom was sitting on the couch talking to Raney. I said hi to my mom and Raney, like I normally did when I came in from outside playing. I proceeded to walk slowly past them to go upstairs. They continued with their conversation. Neither of them looked up to acknowledge my presence in the room or respond to my hello. Here I was worried that I might get in trouble. That was when I realized no one missed me. No one even knew or cared that I had not been home all night. I said to myself that they really did not know that I was gone for twenty-four hours. Although I was a child, I was still shocked that they did not care. I got a weird feeling when that happened. I felt like I was almost invisible to them. But after giving it some thought, I said, "Who cares if they acknowledge me or not. Now I know I am free to go and come as I please, do whatever I want when I want, and Raney's not beating me up." I was good with being invisible. I could always put a positive spin on anything. The dumpster became my refuge. On the warmest nights, I had started spending more nights in the dumpsters. Most of the time, things continued to be chaotic at home. Every chance my sisters got, they would leave and stay with their friends overnight. I did not blame them at all. I would have done the same thing if I had friends to stay with. I just did not have any.

My oldest sister, Lena, was getting frustrated with the way my mom was taking care of us. Lena approached my mom one day when she had reached her boiling point about the lack of care and concern my mom was showing. She felt my mother had stopped trying to take care of us. Later that day, Lena and Mom's conversation turned into a heated argument. Once Lena threatened to tell my grandmother on her, the argument escalated fast. My mom told Lena she needed to stay in a child's place and she needed to shut her mouth and sit down. Lena preceded to challenge my mother about telling our grandmother. They began to yell at each other louder and louder to the point that Lena said, "I am tired of you, and I am going to go tell Gran right now." Lena was standing in the kitchen close to the back door. Lena turned, and it looked like she was getting ready to go out the back door.

The next thing I saw was my mom's fist going across Lena's face. Then my mom yelled out in an angry voice, "You're not going anywhere, young lady." My mom hit Lena so hard she fell straight back on the floor. The kitchen floor was gray concrete, just like all the rest of the floors in the house. For a moment, Lena did not know what happened. When Lena realized my mom had hit her, she got off the floor, crying hysterically and swinging her fists back and forth, trying her best to hit my mom. Then Lena started kicking, punching, and scratching my mom. She scratched my mom all over her arms and face. My mother grabbed Lena around her neck and slung her to the floor. Then mom climbed on top of Lena and pinned her arms down with her knees. She grabbed Lena by her hair and beat her head into the floor until it bled. Lena tried to free herself by attempting to wrestle with my mom. At the same time, Lena continued to scratch my mom all over her face and pulled out a handful of bloody hair from my mom's scalp. The wind was blowing in from the back door, causing the bloody chunks of hair to be blown all the way into the front room. There was blood all over the kitchen floor.

I was screaming at the top of my lungs, "Stop, Mom! Stop, Lena! Please stop!" I yelled repeatedly. Oma and Raney tried to pull them apart, but they were unsuccessful and getting hit in the process. So they stopped trying to help after a few tries and stood back. It was not much longer when Lena realized she was no match for my mother. The moment Lena got off the floor and on her feet, she ran out the back door with her clothes torn half off her and blood running down her back. My mom yelled at her as she was running away, "I hope that teaches you a lesson not to ever raise your hand at me again, and another thing, do not come back until I tell you to!" Lena just kept running, never looking back. Later, I found out Lena went and stayed with a friend of hers for a couple of weeks.

While Lena was gone, I spent a lot of time outside playing by myself until one day, I found a box filled with books in the downstairs closet. The books had pictures on the cover of men and women in a romantic scenes. Most of the book covers had a man carrying a woman, as if he were sweeping her off her feet, while the other book covers looked like the couples were in an argument. I could not read, so I did not have any idea what the books were about other than the pictures on the cover. I asked my mom about the books. She said her last boyfriend left them. I asked her if I could have one, and she said I could have them all, that they reminded her of him, and she wanted them out of the house. The box was too heavy for me to pick up. I needed to figure out a way to get the books out of the house. I remembered one day I saw my neighbor Edna with a red wagon. I hurried next door to ask Edna if I could borrow her wagon, and to my surprise, she said yes. I quickly pulled the wagon to my back door. I started loading up the wagon with the books before my mom changed her mind. I said to myself, "I bet somebody will give me a penny, nickel, or a dime for each of these books." I did not know how to count money, but I was quite sure the store cashier would help me spend it.

After my wagon was fully loaded, I went door to door, pulling my wagon of books. When an adult would come to the door, I told them my mother no longer wanted the books, and I had them for sale. Then I would try to hand them a book to check out. None of the women were interested and told me to go home. They also said I was too young to be going to strangers' houses. Normally, I would be afraid, but for some reason, I had no fear while attempting to sell the books. To my surprise, every man who looked at a book bought one, two, or three. By sunset, I had sold every book in my wagon. One man even smiled and said to come back if I got more. For some reason, that made me feel good about myself, that I had brought joy to a person's life by selling him a book. My little pockets were full of nickels, dimes, and pennies. I did not how much I made, but for a five-year-old, I felt like I was rich. I went to the corner store and bought myself some chips, Hostess Twinkies, and a pop. I had got a taste of sales at five years old, and I liked it.

Meanwhile, Raney was getting closer to my mom while Lena was gone. Lena finally returned home, and when she did, she stayed to herself. I did not hear any more complaints or arguments between her and my mom. During the time Lena was gone, Raney took full advantage of pleasing my mom so she would continue being my mother's favorite child. My mom had started giving Raney more and more authority over the house. As a matter of fact, that was a time when Raney could do no wrong in my mother's eyesight. My mom gave her so much authority over me she had started calling me her personal slave. She said I had to do whatever she told me to do. No matter how bad it was, she said, I had to obey her. Raney used her authority over me to help her terrorize the children in the neighborhood. I hated doing the things she made me do, but if I tried to resist, she just beat me up until I gave in. One night, Raney made me help her take the neighbors' clothes off their clotheslines in the back of their apartment. Most of the time, she would trash their clothes, but occasionally, she would find something she really liked. Then she would boldly wear it the next day in front of the owner's house. If the owner tried to confront her in any way with a threat, Raney would wait outside their house until nightfall. If one of the little girls who lived there came back outside after dinner, Raney would catch them, hold them down, and cut off their ponytail. She said she got the idea from the Indians. She saw how they scalped their enemies on TV.

I hated being around her because she was such a bully. Every chance I got, I would leave the house. First thing in the morning, I would get myself together, then go and search of a friend and some food. I thought if I found a friend, I would have someone to play with and spend the night with. The dumpsters were no longer safe. The last time I tried to spend the night in the dumpster, I had almost got towed away. On that day, the trash was too low. Once I climbed in it, I could barely reach the opening to get myself back out. When the truck came to pick up the dumpster that day, I was still trying to get out when it began to move. I said to myself, "I could die in here." That scared me so bad I did not ever go back into the dumpsters again.

CHAPTER 4

. . . .

New Friends and Fun

It was a beautiful sunny day when I decided to go for a walk. I walked from one project building to another. I was bored and tired of playing by myself. Halfway into my walk, I saw a little girl who looked to be around my age playing in the dirt. I walked up to her and asked her if I could play with her. She said yes and that she was tired of playing by herself. She said her name was Shirley Pittman. Shirley only lived about four or five buildings away from my building. Once Shirley and I started talking and playing, there was no stopping us. It looked like I had found that friend I had been looking for. We had fun playing in the dirt and making mud pies, and we drew designs in the dirt using sticks. Shirley said she also had a ball and jacks in a pouch in her pocket. I asked, "What are jacks?"

She replied, "Let me show you." She poured the jacks and the ball on the ground. The jacks looked like some kind of small metal stars. The ball was small, soft, and red. Shirley said, "I will teach you how to play." It was fun and easy even for a five-year-old. All I had to do was sit on the ground, get a handful of jacks, toss them on the ground in front of me, throw the ball in the air, and pick up a jack before the ball bounced twice. We played jacks until it was almost dark.

Shirley took me to her house so I could meet her mother. I was more than happy to meet her family. I was hoping that I could possibly become part of it. Shirley's mom was single, and her name was Ms.

Pittman. Her mom also had two sons named Jack and Larry. Shirley's family was very hospitable to me. I did not want to leave and return to my house. I asked Shirley to ask her mom if I could spend the night. Shirley's mom answered and said, "You must ask your mother first." I said okay and immediately ran home to ask my mom. Of course, my mother said yes. Even though I had just met Shirley that day, Ms. Pittman agreed and let me spend the night. Shirley and I got along like sisters. We were so close after only knowing each other for a few weeks. Shirley said she had always wanted a sister whom she could talk and play with. We began doing everything together. Kick ball, dodgeball, and hide-and-seek—Shirley knew all kinds of games; I thought her brothers taught her most of them.

Shirley was full of surprises. One day, she told me that she knew a place where crystal stones were piled as high as mountains. "What is a crystal? And where is this place?" I asked.

She said, "A crystal is a clear rock that looks like a big diamond that you can hold in your hand. You have to see it for yourself. It is hard to explain."

I asked, "Can we go there right now?"

She said, "Yes, just let me tell my mom that we're going walking."

Her mom said okay.

We took off walking, and it seemed like we were walking forever. Finally, we reached the entrance to a big company. I saw a couple of large trucks dumping something onto a large pile on the ground. I asked Shirley if that was the mountain she spoke about earlier. She replied, "Yes, those are the crystals, but the mountain looked a lot bigger last time." There were smaller trucks hauling the crystals away from the company.

I asked Shirley, "Will we get in trouble going on the property with the trucks?"

She replied, "No. Just stay out the way of the trucks, and the workers do not care. They told me and my brothers last time to take all we want."

So Shirley and I entered the property and walked past the workers and right up to the big hill of crystals. Wow, she was not lying! The first crystal I picked up was bigger than my hand. It was just like

Shirley said. The crystals looked like big chunks of glass with sharp points on each end. We hurried up and stuffed our pockets and had a few in our hands. It was so simple and easy, and we were on our way. Just as we were leaving the property, one of the young men working yelled out, asking us what we were planning to do with all those salt rocks. "What salt rocks?" I asked while looking at Shirley, puzzled.

He replied, "The salt rocks in your hands."

I stopped walking and asked him, "What is a salt rock?"

He explained that the rocks had been dug out of a mountain and brought there for shipment. He went on to say that those rocks get ground up and put on the streets when it snowed. I got so mad when he said that. I thought I had something special. I took most the salt rocks out of my pockets and threw them on the ground. I was so disappointed. On the way home, I got hungry and wanted to know what a salt rock tasted like. I started licking it, and it did not taste too bad. It tasted just like the salt in my house, but for some reason, I liked this better. Shirley and I made it back home safely with our crystal salt rocks. Shirley went to her house, and I went to mine. The next day, when I awoke hungry, I thought about my salt rock. I began licking on the salt rock like a popsicle until I was not hungry anymore. Eventually, I started using the salt rock to suppress my hunger pains. I became dependent on it. It got to the point I did not go anywhere without my rock. I got a couple of extra salt rocks from Shirley just to make sure I did not run out.

It was not long before I was back trying to spend as many nights over at Shirley's house as I could. Then one day, Ms. Pittman said she wanted to meet my mother. She said that I had spent a lot of nights at their house, and it was time for her to meet my mother. She told me to tell my mom that she wanted to meet her. Ms. Pittman said, "Tell her we can meet at her house or mine." My mom agreed and decided it was easier for Ms. Pittman to our house. Once my mom and Ms. Pittman met, they clicked like they knew each other all along. I thought, "Great, I will be able to spend more time over Shirley's house. Now that my mom had a good friend to talk to, she would be happy, like me." But my mom had a boyfriend named Mr. Thomas. He really did not like my mom having any company at our house or having friends, so that caused friction with Ms. Pittman and Mr. Thomas. Eventually, Ms. Pittman stopped coming around, but she still let me spend some nights with them.

After a couple of months had passed, Shirley and I were playing in the streets, throwing rocks and trying to see who could throw the farthest. And out of the blue, Shirley started talking about my mother. She was saying things like "You know, your mother's nasty."

I asked, "Why did you say my mother's nasty?"

She said, "Because my mother told me your mother's nasty. And my mother does not like your mother because your mother sleeps with all kinds of men."

I asked Shirley, "What do you mean my mother sleeps with all kinds of men?"

She said, "Your mom does the nasty with all kinds of men."

I did not really know what Shirley was talking about, but it hurt me to hear her say nasty things about my mother. I asked Shirley, "Stop talking about my mother, please."

Shirley just began to say more and more bad things concerning my mother and laughing while she was saying it. I asked her again to please stop talking about my mother, and instead of stopping, she called my mom a whore. I did not know what a whore was, but the way she said it, I knew it was something bad. Then Shirley said, "A whore is a nasty person."

I started crying, asking Shirley to please stop talking about my mother and calling her names. I did not know why it hurt me so bad to hear her say those things about my mom. I just knew I needed her to stop right then, not one more word. When Shirley saw me get more and more agitated, she began laughing so hard that she was bending over holding her stomach and laughing. All I remembered after that was seeing a long barbecue pitchfork lying in the gutter in the street next to the curb. I grabbed the fork and stuck it right between Shirley's eyes. I stuck the pitchfork in her face so hard that she could not pull it out. There were two streams of blood running down her face under her eyes, onto her cheeks, and down on the ground. It scared me so bad I screamed; I could not believe I did that. I yelled out, "Oh my god! Shirley, I am so sorry!"

Shirley started screaming, "Why did you do this to me?" She was crying and yelling, "I cannot see! I cannot see!"

I reached toward her face to try to pull the fork out of her face, but she would not let me get close to her. She was wiping her eyes, trying to see the direction of her house. As soon as she got a glimpse of her project building, she took off running in that direction. As she ran to her house, I knew I was in big trouble. I ran to my house to tell my mom what had happened before anybody else could tell her. I explained to her how Shirley was talking about her and how I defended her name by shutting Shirley up. I told my mother I did not want to hurt Shirley. I just could not take her laughing and talking bad about her. My mom asked, "Where Shirley is now?" I told her she had ran home to tell her mother.

Before I could say another word, Ms. Pittman was beating on our front door. My mom opened the door. Ms. Pittman was yelling, saying, "Your daughter just tried to put my daughter's eyes out with a pitchfork." She said Shirley was on her way to the hospital, and we better hoped there was no damage to her eyes. She said the paramedics said the prongs of the fork barely missed both her eyes. I was standing in the front room with tears rolling down my face, thinking about what I had done and how could I do that to my friend. Then on the other hand, I was worried about what my mom would do to me and what kind of beating I would get for this.

I was hoping that my mom would understand how bad it hurt me when Shirley called her those names and she would rule on my defense and give me a light punishment. Instead, she took Ms. Pittman's advice and ruled for me to be punished severely, saying somebody had got to teach me a lesson while I was still young. My mom agreed and promised Ms. Pittman that I would get a harsh punishment. Then she apologized while asking Ms. Pittman if there was anything she could do to help Shirley to just let her know. Then she repeated, "Lane is going to get a punishment that she will never forget. Because when I get through with her, she won't ever do anything like this again." I had no idea what my mom was planning, but I was about to find out.

CHAPTER 5

. . . .

On My Deathbed

As soon as Ms. Pittman left from the house, my mother called my sister Raney and said to me, "Lane, you have left me with no other choice but to let your sister Raney discipline you." Then she said, "Raney, she is all yours. Punish her however you like."

Raney immediately grabbed me. I tried pushing her hands off me as I attempted to get loose from her, but she was too strong. I thought I would have just ran away that day and never came back if I could have got loose from her especially if I had any idea what was coming next. Raney had me by the neck and started pulling me toward the stairs. I tried fighting her, but she had put me in a headlock using both her arms. She started dragging me by my hair and neck up the stairs. She said, "When I get you up the stairs, you are really going to get it." Then she stopped and smiled at me and said, "I am going to hurt you."

I started screaming for my mom, "Please, Mom, please do not let her hurt me. I promise I will not be bad anymore. I promise. I am so sorry for what I did to Shirley."

My mom yelled out, "Shut up! Raney, go ahead and take care of her and shut her up."

As soon as Raney got me into the bedroom, she shut the door. She began kicking and beating me with her fists and elbows. She was hitting me with all her strength. Then she pushed me in the corner of the room and told me to stay there while she went to get some ropes.

When she left to get the ropes, I was wiping my face, trying to stop my nose and lip from bleeding. I was also trying to figure out how I could run past Raney and my mom and get out of the house, but Raney found some ropes and returned before I could make a move. She made me take off all my clothes except my underwear. We were in the bedroom at the end of the hall. This room had a black metal bed frame with four black metal posts, two at the top and two at the bottom. In the center of the full-size bed frame were black coil bed springs. There was no mattress, pillows, or bed covers, just the metal springs. A dresser and mirror were on the opposite side of the bed against the wall, and a large window was above the dresser. Raney was still hitting and kicking me all over my body and, at the same time, telling me to be still. She threatened to get the extension cord again if I did not hold still. By now, my nose had stopped bleeding, and my face was covered in tears and snot. My eyes were swollen, and my ribs hurt from all the kicking. I was tired of fighting and blocking the blows. She had worn me down.

The first thing Raney did was tie one end of the rope to my wrist, then she tied the other end of the rope to the bedpost. She pulled the rope extremely tight. Then she continued to tie my other wrist, then my ankles to the bottom bedpost. Raney pulled the ropes so tight that it raised my body up and off the springs until only my bottom barely touched the coil springs. Because my body was so small, I was suspended in the air. Raney told me she was going to leave me tied up when she went downstairs and I better kept my mouth shut. As soon as I thought she was downstairs, I started yelling, "Somebody, anybody, help me!" I cried out again, saying, "Anybody, please, can you hear me?" I hoped maybe one of our neighbors would hear my cries for help.

Then Raney yelled up the stairs and said, "If you do not shut up, I am going to beat you some more!"

Feeling helpless and tied up like an animal, I decided to shut up. Plus, I was out of breath from all the crying and yelling. As I laid there, I was trying to figure out how to free myself, and I was hoping Rosie would be home soon. But unfortunately, I had remembered Rosie was spending the weekend with a friend for a few days. I was so exhausted and frustrated especially after I remembered Rosie was not coming home for a few days. I just cried myself to sleep.

When I awoke, I began working hard in twisting my arms back and forth again and again, trying unsuccessfully to free myself. I was left there all night, and when dawn came, the sun shined right into my face. There were no curtains, blinds, shades, or any covering over the window. Unfortunately, the window was too high for anyone to see me being abused in my bedroom from the outside. I tried twisting my little wrist out of the ropes until the ropes cut into my skin, and my wrist started to bleed. Once I saw that my wrist were bleeding, I started screaming and crying and screaming and crying all over again. I had to pee. I needed to go to the bathroom really bad, and I was hungry and thirsty too. When I started screaming, Raney ran in my room and told me to shut up. I also told her I was cold, my arms hurt, and they had started bleeding again. I begged her to please forgive me and untie me. She started laughing and then spoke, saying, "You can pee right where you are. And I am not giving you any food or water to eat. And you are not getting a blanket or a pillow. As matter of fact, for making me come back up here and talk to you, I am going to give you another whipping." She whipped me this time with a belt. I could not shut up. I was hoping maybe one of my older sisters, like Lena or Ommie, might come to my rescue. Or maybe someone from next door could hear my cries, call the police, and get me untied.

Raney said she had had enough of me at this point, and she was going to fix my big mouth. When Raney said she was going to fix my mouth, I knew she was planning something bad. So as soon as she went back downstairs, I started screaming again with all my might. I was yelling things like, "Help me! I am a child tied up in the bedroom. They are beating me, and I am not being fed. Help me! Someone, please!" I was hoping that I would catch somebody's attention next door. Well, it caught someone's attention all right. It caught my mom's attention downstairs. I heard my mom yell to Raney, "You are going to have to do something to shut her up before someone calls the police."

Raney got the bright idea to put a sock in my mouth to shut me up. She got a regular, old white bobby sock. She rolled it up until the size was a little bigger than a Hostess Twinkie. Then she stuffed it in my mouth. It stretched my mouth open so wide I was gagging, and it was so dry. I was already thirsty. Now I had to contend with a thick sock in my mouth. On top of everything else, I had to cough, and I sure could not yell for help anymore. I started crying again. Tears just rolled down the side of my face. The sock was causing me to gag, so I had to stop crying. I was afraid that I would choke to death on the sock. I started thinking it was a great possibility I could die accidentally while being punished at the young age of five. So that was when I started thinking about what my grandmother taught me. She said someday, I might be in a position where only God could help me. If I called on him in the time of trouble, he would never leave me, and he would answer my prayers. So at the age of five, I began my first real prayer, "Oh God, please send someone to untie me and set me free from these ropes." I prayed, and I cried silently to keep from choking on the sock. I prayed through the day and through the night. Another day had come and gone with no help in sight. All I could do was pray and watch the sun rise and set. I had urinated on myself a few times. I could hear the pee hitting the floor. It had made a puddle underneath me and began to smell. It was going on the third day when my body became so weak and exhausted from the lack of food and water. And the fact that the ropes were so tight, each pulling in a different direction and keeping me suspended in midair, did not help. I prayed and cried until I could not do either anymore.

I was just about to give up and accept my fate that I was going to die right there, tied like a dog on top of some metal springs in my own house with my mom and my sister right downstairs. It was at that time when I heard my sister Rosie's voice. I thought I was hearing things or having a dream or something, but it was my prayers being answered. When I heard her voice downstairs, I knew it was Rosie. I heard her say, "Where is Laney?"

Raney replied, "She is not here."

Rosie said, "Well, where is she, then?"

Raney said, "I do not know. She is gone."

At that time, I started trying to make some kind of noise so Rosie could hear me. I was hoping to get her attention so she would come upstairs and check out the situation and find me. With that sock in my mouth, I could not do much of anything but moan and groan. I was making all kinds of moaning and groaning sounds as loud as I could. I tried to shake the bed with my body, but I did not have enough strength to move. Somehow, I evidently made enough moaning sounds that Rosie heard something. I heard Rosie ask Raney, "What was that sound upstairs?"

Raney said, "Oh, that is nothing. You should go back outside and play."

Rosie said, "No there is something wrong. Where is Lane?" Right then Rosie said, "Move aside. I am going upstairs." Raney tried to block her from going upstairs. That was when Rosie pushed Raney real hard and knocked her to the floor. Raney was no match for Rosie. Rosie could win a fight every time. As Rosie ran up the stairs, I could hear her opening the bedroom doors as she got closer to the room that I was in. When she got to my room and opened the door and saw me tied like an animal, she almost fell to the floor. Rosie yelled out in horror. It hurt her so bad to see me like that. She yelled out, "Oh my god, what is going on? Why are you tied up like this?"

I could not speak. I had that sock still in my mouth. I made a couple of groans, and she ran over to me and pulled the sock out of my mouth. I could hardly move my jaws to talk when she removed the sock. Then words finally came to my mouth. I yelled out, crying, "Raney did this to me. Raney tied me up, and Raney beat me."

Rosie started crying and shaking. She was so angry. She tried to untie my arms, but the ropes were too tight. When she saw how deep the ropes had cut into my wrist, she told me not to move. The more she tried to loosen the ropes, the deeper they went into my skin. She saw that she would not be able to break the rope with her bare hands. She said she had to go downstairs and get something to cut the ropes. She said she promised me she would be right back. Her voice was trembling and cracking as she was speaking. She continued to say with tears streaming down her face, "I will be right back. I promise you." I never saw Rosie so angry. Then she turned to go get a knife from the kitchen.

I yelled out, "Rosie, please do not leave me!"

She was yelling "I will be right back!" as she was running down the stairs. Raney was waiting on Rosie when she came downstairs. I could hear her trying to convince Rosie that my punishment was justified. Rosie did not want to hear anything Raney had to say and told her if she did not get out of her face, she was going to hurt her. Rosie then got the knife and ran back upstairs. I could hear her yell out to Raney, "Do not come upstairs. I do not want to hurt you, Raney." Rosie started cutting the ropes loose until I was free of all of them. She tried to lift me off the springs. I did not have the strength to pull myself up. As much as I wanted to get off that bed and run out of that room, I could hardly move. As Rosie slowly got me in position to be able to sit up and lower my legs to the floor, tears were running down both our faces. Rosie was breathing deeply, trying to clear her throat to say, "I got to get you into the bathroom. And I must get you some food and water." Rosie pulled me off the bed and slung my arm around her neck. She struggled to pull and sometimes drag my feet to the bathroom down the hall.

When we finally got to the bathroom, she had me sit on the toilet and hang my arms over the sink. She ran warm water over my wrist, trying to rinse off the dried blood and small scabs that had formed. Then she used a washcloth and bar soap and began washing my wrist and my ankles. It hurt so bad, but she said she had to get them clean, or I would get an infection. Rosie suddenly yelled out to Raney, "You better not ever put your hands on Lane again!" Rosie continued to say, "I promise you, if you ever touch her again, I will hurt you." And then Rosie turned to me and said, "I will never leave you by yourself overnight with Mama and Raney again," and she did not.

CHAPTER 6

. . . .

Running Away

After the punishment, several months went by without any major incidents. I stayed to myself because I was no longer interested in having a friend. I became Rosie's shadow, following her wherever she went. It seemed like it was not long before my mom had another boyfriend. When mom introduced my sisters and I to her new boy-friend, Mr. Williams, I got the feeling he didn't like kids. The way he looked at me made me feel uncomfortable. He had a mean look, like he wanted to whip me for no reason at all. I did my best to stay away from him. My sister Raney did not like him either, but she took a different approach. She began asking Mr. Williams a lot of ques-tions and voicing her opinion concerning his relationship with our mother. Things really got heated when he raised his voice at Raney, and my mom did not stop him. As time went by, Raney directed her complaints to our mother. She told our mother that she was spending too much time with Mr. Williams and not paying me and my sisters any attention. That conversation angered my mom, and for the first time, Raney was no longer my mom's favorite child. Their arguments were becoming more and more frequent and intense until one day when my mom and her boyfriend were sitting on the couch talking and Raney interrupted their conversation. My mom told Raney to go outside and play. Raney yelled back to mom, "That is it! I have had it with you and your boyfriend. I am tired of you not paying me any attention!" Then she said, "I am going to tell Gran on you."

That was when Mom felt like Raney had crossed the line as a child. My mother did not like people who were tattletales. That was something she despised. My mother yelled out to Raney, "You better shut your mouth, or I will shut it for you."

Raney repeated again that she had enough. Then she suddenly grabbed me by my arm and neck and said, "We're running away right now. We are going to Gran's house."

I replied, "But I do not want to go. I want to stay here with Rosie. Please turn me loose." Rosie had gone to the store with a friend earlier and had not made it back.

Then Raney hit me with her hand and told me to shut my mouth. She yanked my arm and pulled me out the back door. Before I could stop her, we were outside on the sidewalk. She started yelling "Run!" repeatedly. She said, "Run faster I said," as she was pulling me down the sidewalk. My legs were getting tangled up as I was having a problem keeping up. Every time I was about to fall, she would yank me up before my knees hit the ground. She started slapping me on the back of the head, saying, "Hurry up, slowpoke." Before I knew it, we were a couple of blocks away from the house. I finally gave up struggling with her once we had gotten a long distance from the house. Raney finally got tired of running and decided to slow down so we could catch our breath. As we slowed down, I started looking at all the pretty flowers in the different yards. Raney began talking to me about all kinds of things, like I was her best friend. I guess she just needed someone to talk to. I was not interested in being her friend or listening to anything she had to say. I had not forgotten about the punishment she gave me on the bed.

After a lot of talking and walking, it had begun to get dark. We had been walking for a few hours. Raney said she hoped she had not gotten the directions mixed up. I asked her, "What do you mean? Are we lost?"

She replied, "No, we just got to go back the way we came and make a couple of turns."

I did not know a lot about directions, but I knew that sounded like we were lost. That was when I got scared. I was thinking all kinds of thoughts. My imagination was going crazy.

Raney and I continued to look and walk for hours until it was almost eleven at night. Raney finally gave up and said, "Lane, we are lost. We are going to have to knock on a stranger's door and ask for help." I tried telling her that was not a good idea because it was so late at night. Raney told me to shut it up and that she had it all figured out. She said, "Once they call Gran and tell her we are lost, Gran will come and pick us up." So Raney made a desperate decision to choose a house on the block that we were standing at. Raney chose a small brick home that sat back among the trees with a fence around it. The fence had a gate with a metal handle. We had to lift the handle and pull the gate toward us to enter. All the lights were off inside and outside. If it were not for the streetlight and a full moon shining, it would have been pitch black. We slowly walked inside the yard and up a few steps on to the wooden porch. Raney gently knocked on the screen door a couple of times and waited. There was no response. Then she knocked very firm several times. I began to shake. I was terrified on who might answer the door.

Suddenly, we heard a lot of movement inside the house. Then the curtains started moving, and then a face peeked through the curtain. It was an elderly white man's voice that yelled out, asking, "Who are you and what do you want?"

Raney said in a loud, trembling voice, "Sir, we are two children lost."

The porch light came on as the man slowly cracked the door. He opened the door a little bit more to see who we were. Then he called to his wife and said, "Honey, come here. There are two little colored girls out here on the porch alone. They said that they are lost."

His wife came to the door and saw how frightened we looked. She yelled out, "Oh, my goodness! Dear, look at the little one. She looks scared to death." Then she said, "Open the door and let them in."

As soon as we got in the house, they started asking all kinds of questions. The lady was concerned if we were cold, thirsty, or hungry. The man was concerned with our safety. He was asking Raney all kinds of questions, like why we were out at that time of the night, why we were by ourselves, where were our parents. Raney had no problem answering their questions and giving them more information about my mom than they asked for. Raney knew the stuff that she was telling the couple were personal and would make my mom look like a bad mother. Finally, Raney ask the lady if she would call my grandparents and ask her to please come and pick us up. The lady replied, "Sure. What is your grandmother's phone number?" They had one of those big, heavy black phones that you stuck your finger in the hole and pull the circle halfway around until it got to the number. It was a little different than my grandparents' phone, which hung on the wall. After they reached my grandparents and had a brief conversation with them, my grandparents were on their way to come and get us. Once my grandparents arrived and saw that we were unharmed and being taken incredibly good care of, they were more thankful than angry, considering that we had ran away from home. Before we left the house, Gran was thanking the couple for their kind words and their hospitality that they extended to us. We all said our goodbyes and got into the station wagon.

Once we got into the station wagon, my grandparents did not hold back how upset they really were with my mother. Raney told them everything that was going on in our household, and it made my grandparents incredibly angry. My grandmother explained that we would be staying with them for the night, but they would be taking us back in the morning. The next day, as we were riding back to the projects, my grandmother said she was going to have a long talk with our mother. When we got back home, my mother was waiting on us at the front door. She was upset and wanted to know how we got to our grandparents' house. She asked in an angry voice why we didn't tell her we were going to Gran's house. Raney went to yell out some words, but before she could say anything, my grandmother told us to go outside and play because she needed to have a private conversation with our mother. At the completion of an awfully long talk with my mom, my grandmother called me and my sisters together to tell us that they would be back to check on us every week. She gave us all her phone number to call if we had any kind of emergency.

CHAPTER 7

. . . .

From the House to the Hospital

My grandmother kept her word, checking up on us every week and making sure we were okay. But as time went by, the checking on us got to be less frequent. It went from one week of checking to every two weeks of checking to about a month or more apart. When the checking got to be about a month or two apart, things began to worsen. Mom was back having problems dealing with everyday tasks, like cooking and cleaning and caring for us. Then one day, to all our surprise, there was a knock on the front door. We were all sitting around downstairs, minding our own business. Raney had just finished cooking a stack of bacon grease sandwiches. The sandwiches consisted of bread and bacon grease. The grease would accumulate after a few weeks of cooking the bacon. Then we would pour the fat in a big, empty can. They were easy to make. Just pour the grease in a hot skillet and brown it on both sides. Yummy, they tasted so good!

My mom got up and answered the door. There was a large number of white people standing outside our door. A lady dressed like she was going to church spoke up and said, "Let me introduce myself and my coworkers. We have been sent from child protection services to remove and place your children in foster care."

Then a man and two ladies dressed like doctors and nurses in all white with white shoes on stepped in front of the welfare lady and said, "My name is Mr. Green. Myself and my two assistants are here on behalf of the state of Colorado. We have been assigned to remove you from your home and deliver you to the Colorado state mental institution for psychological evaluation."

My mother was outraged and began yelling at them, demanding that they all leave and get off her property right now. She continued yelling, saying she was not going anywhere with them, period, and no one better not touch her children.

Then Mr. Green said, "I am sorry, Mrs. Manning, but if you refuse to cooperate, we will have to restrain you. And it would be nice if we could avoid that in front of the children."

That really made my mom mad when he mentioned restraining her. She said, "No one is restraining me, and like I said, all of you need to get back in your cars and leave now." She was shouting, "Move out of my doorway so I can shut the door."

Mr. Green leaned into the door and stuck his foot between the door so my mom could not shut it. My mom reached her arm out to push him out of the doorway. And that's when things got ugly real fast. Mr. Green grabbed my mother's arm and pulled her out of the house. The two ladies who looked like nurses jumped in and started helping him restrain my mom. They were working together, like it was a well-rehearsed plan. Before my mother knew what was happening, she was in that white jacket. She struggled, trying to free her arms, but she could not move them. There were two long belts that were attached. They tied the two belts in the back of her jacket. My mom was so angry she was kicking, crying, and yelling all kinds of things, saying, "Please do not take my children, please. I beg you. They're all I got." Then she would go back to yelling and cursing at the people, saying, "You better get this thing off my body." Then my mom said, "Girls, go call your grandmother and tell her what is going on."

Then Mr. Green said, "I am afraid that will not help you, Mrs. Manning. Her name is on the bottom of this order."

My mom said, "What!"

"I said your mom called the authorities on you."

My mom was so devastated by that statement she stopped fighting and surrendered. She calmed down and allowed them to help her into the back of the white wagon. There were two small windows at the back of the truck, one on each door. I could see my mom's face through the windows as she sat and waited until they were ready to leave. The female social workers explained to me and my sisters that our mother was sick, and my grandmother asked them to get her some help. I said she did not look sick to me, but if my grandmother asked them to take care of my mom and take her to the hospital, she must have trusted them to help my mom. So I decided not to question their explanation why they were taking her to the hospital any further. The ladies instructed me and my sisters to go and get our favorite toy or doll because we would be leaving the house, and it would be a long time before we return.

One of the ladies told us that their main job was to place children in foster care. Lena, my oldest sister, asked where we were going. The social worker said, "You would have gone directly to a foster home, but due to your living conditions and your shot records not being up-to-date, we must place all of you in the hospital first. Each of you will undergo a physical and get your vaccination shots. Because now that you all are property of the state of Colorado, the state has the responsibility to make sure you're healthy enough to be placed in the foster care system." So we all picked out our toy or doll and followed the ladies into the two cars parked in front of the house. The neighbors were standing in the yards, looking at us. I think they thought my mom was going to jail because when she refused to cooperate, it looked like she was under some type of arrest.

When we arrived at the hospital, the first thing they did was give us a bath and told us to put on some little white gowns they gave us. They said that the hospital rooms were full, so Rosie and I had to sleep in the beds placed in the hallways. My other sisters were in the hospital rooms not far from us down the hall. There were a lot of empty beds in the hallway, but we were the only ones sleeping in them. The beds looked like large white baby beds with bars around all four sides that you could lift in the middle. I did not mind being placed in the hallway or in the baby bed. I kind of liked it. I could see all the people coming and going. There was a lady who came around with food on a tray. The trays were stacked on top of a cart. She offered me lunch and told me she would be back with dinner later.

I thought this was a great place, and I hoped my mom's hospital was just as nice. For the first time in a long time, I had clean clothes, a bath, and food all in the same day. Even though I was a little scared, I really liked staying in the hospital. We stayed in the hospital for about a week or until they found each one of us foster homes.

CHAPTER 8

. . . .

A New Home Brings New Challenges

The social workers talked about separating each one of us and came to a decision that they thought it would be in my best interest to stay with Rosie since I was so close to her. I was the youngest who would cling to Rosie for dear life. My other sisters were placed separately in individual foster homes. The first foster home Rosie and I went to was with a white lady named Mrs. Tucker. She had a medium build with long brown hair. I did not know why, but she seemed to be angry. We did not see Mr. Tucker, and we did not ask where he was. Rosie and I slept in bunk beds in a small room located toward the back of their home. It was a one-story house, not fancy but not raggedy.

On the very first night, Mrs. Tucker warned us repeatedly, "Do not wet the bed." Wetting the bed was something I never had a problem with. So I did not think much about what she was saying. At bedtime, Mrs. Tucker gave us a big glass of Kool-Aid right before we went to bed. She told us to drink it all up. It was my first time having Kool-Aid. All I knew was it was so good. I not only drank mine, but I also drank half of Rosie's. Then in the middle of the night, I awoke having the need to go to the bathroom. I looked around the room, and all the lights were out. The bathroom was down a long hallway. It was so dark. I got up and tried to walk in the direction of the bathroom, but it was too dark. I was too afraid to venture down that long, dark hallway. I said to myself, "I am going to have to hold it." And I went and got back into bed. I drifted back off to sleep, and somewhere between me getting back in the bed and morning, I wet the bed. I knew I was in big trouble, so I tried to hide it by making the bed up. I covered up the spot as though nothing had happened. Mrs. Tucker called for us to come and get our breakfast. We got up, brushed our teeth, and washed up. We went to the kitchen and was given our seating arrangement. On the table was a big bowl of corn-flakes waiting for each one of us. Just as I was about to get a mouthful of good old cornflakes and milk, I heard Mrs. Tucker yell out, "Who slept on the bottom bunk?" Rosie pointed to me. I knew exactly what was going on and what she was getting ready to say. She yelled out, "Elaine, did you wet the bed last night?"

I said, "Yes, ma'am. I tried to get up, but it was dark. I tried to hold it until daylight, but I fell asleep, and that is when it happened."

She said, "For that, you will eat cornflakes for the rest of the week with water." She took my bowl of cornflakes that had milk. She poured me another bowl of cornflakes, then held the bowl over the sink and ran cold water on my cornflakes. At least she allowed me to add sugar, and that helped. I was so hungry I ate them just like they had milk, but it was not the same. I ate my cereal like that every day we were at that foster home. I did not drink any more Kool-Aid at bedtime. We were only there for about a week. When Mrs. Tucker called our social worker and told her that Rosie and I were eating her out of her house and home, she said that she did not want to keep us any longer. So we packed up our things and was off to our second foster home in less than two weeks.

CHAPTER 9

. . . .

Leave Your Judgment
at the Door

The next foster home we were placed in was with an interracial couple. Their house was an old, worn-out house. The wife told us to call her by her nickname Red. She said she got her nickname because of her bright scarlet-red hair. She did not have any teeth in her mouth. I found it interesting listening to the way she would pronounce her words. Later, I found out she was from the South. The reason she talked differently was because she had a Southern accent. Her husband's name was Henry, and Henry was a Black man. He had no outstanding features that stood out other than the way he was dressed. He was dressed like a farmer with blue overalls on. He welcomed us to their home with his arms stretched out and a big smile, attempting to hug both of us. His hands were covered in dirt, as if he had been digging or planting something. He said, "Welcome to your temporary home. You can relax now. No one is going to hurt you here." He went on to say there were two other children staying with them, but they had just left earlier in the day.

Their house was exceedingly small and cluttered with so much junk. Rosie and I both slept in the same bed, which could barely fit in the room. The following morning, when they called us to breakfast, we would all sit around the table and bow our heads for prayer. In the center of the table was a large mixing bowl, like my grandmother used to make cakes. The bowl was filled full of cornflakes and milk. It seemed like cornflakes was the standard breakfast food for foster homes. We were each given a spoon and a bowl and told to dig in. Whoever ate the fastest ate the most. It seemed a little weird, but I was too hungry to complain. Plus, I could eat fast.

You could tell they did not have a lot of money. I wondered why they were taking in so many foster kids when they were struggling themselves. Later, I was told that they were an emergency facility. The children living with them were only supposed to stay a week or two just until a more permanent foster home could be found. We lived with Red and Henry for about a week. When it was time to leave, Henry and Red told us we were good girls, and they hoped we would get a nice foster home to live in. They also said our social worker would be coming to pick me and Rosie up in the morning. The next morning, we got up and ate our cornflakes and milk again from the big breakfast bowl, as usual. Then Rosie and I started preparing for our departure to our next foster home. Our social worker arrived, and Rosie and I had our plastic bags full of our belongings. We were ready to go to our next home. Red and Henry gave us a big hug and complimented us on our good behavior to our social worker. Then they told us to take care of ourselves as we loaded our bags into our social worker's car.

CHAPTER 10

. . . .

The Third Foster Home

Rosie and I were now on our way to another foster home. This made our third home in less than three weeks. We're both hoping that we could stay in this home at least until our mom got out of the hospital. On the drive over to our new foster home, Mrs. Booker tried to give us a little insight on our new family. She said their house was located in Southwest Denver. It was a long, interesting drive; we passed a couple of huge companies. One was Montgomery Ward, and another was a big tire company called Gate's Rubber Company. As we passed Gate's Rubber Company, there was a terrible smell. Mrs. Booker said the smell was coming from the burning rubber that they used to make the tires for cars. As she continued driving, she said our new foster parents had two biological teenage boys of their own and a young foster girl around seven or eight years old. Finally, we arrived at our new foster home. The neighborhood reminded me of my grandmother's neighborhood with dirt country roads. I saw a trailer home across the street and a white man sitting on his porch smoking a cigarette. As far as I could see, most of the other houses were single-level brick homes a good distance apart from one another.

As Rosie and I gathered our bags, Mrs. Booker opened the gate. It was a chain-link fence that surrounded the large yard and a large one-story house. A tall heavy-set Black lady came to the door, and then her husband, tall and thin built, walked up behind her. They welcomed us into their home and introduced themselves to us as

Mama and Papa Lottie. Mrs. Booker said it looked like her work was done here, so she would be on her way. Mama Lottie said, "Girls, let me show you to your room." It was a small room with a gigantic bed that was so large I had trouble climbing up on it. But I loved the smell of the clean sheets, and the mattress was so soft.

CHAPTER 11

. . . .

So Many Rules

While we were putting away our things, I asked Mama Lottie, "Where are your sons and the little girl that Mrs. Booker said lived here?"

Mama Lottie said, "The little girl you are talking about is in her room right across the hall from your bedroom. And my sons are in the basement, where their bedrooms are located."

I asked her, "Can we go into the little girl's room and meet her?"

She said the little girl's room was off limits for us. We were under no circumstances permitted to enter her room. She said, "She is being taken good care of, but she never leaves her room." She went on to say, "While we are on the subject of rules, another place that you are not allowed to go is the basement for any reason." Then she asked, "Do you understand me?"

We nodded and said, "Yes, Mama Lottie."

She continued to say, "As long as you obey the rules of this house, you girls will not have any problems." Mama Lottie asked if we were hungry. We answered yes, and we went into the kitchen. She prepared us a peanut butter and jelly sandwich and a glass of milk. When we finished eating, we went in the front room to sit and talk. Their furniture was beautiful. They had a white couch and two white chairs covered in clear plastic with no TV or radio in sight. The reason Mama Lottie called us in to the front room was to get more familiar with us. She asked us lots of questions about our mom and how our living conditions were. When we finished with our conversation, Mama Lottie said, "It is now time for you girls to meet my sons." She walked to the basement door and yelled out, "Boys, come up and meet your foster sisters."

The first one to emerge from the basement was her son named Jack. He was a tall, dark-skinned young man with a thin build and a short haircut. Mama Lottie said her other son's name was Todd. Looking at Todd was just like looking at Jack. Todd was just a little younger and shorter. Both boys seemed to be standoffish. Once we all said our hellos, Todd and Jack went back in the basement.

CHAPTER 12

. . . .

Slave Work

Mama Lottie said, "Now that everyone has gotten familiar with each other, girls, we can get started preparing dinner." She said, "There is always work that needs to be done around here. And believe me, you girls will be busy every day, making sure it gets done. So first, let us get busy peeling some potatoes and carrots for tonight's dinner." She taught us how to peel the potatoes and carrots safely without cutting ourselves. Once we got everything prepped for dinner, we continued working. We got a lesson on how to wash a load of clothes. She showed us how to fill the washing machine up with water using the garden hose from outside, and she would add hot water from the kitchen. After the clothes were finished being washed, we had to drain the water using the black rubber hose attached at the bottom of the washer. Then we had to fill it back up with clean rinse water. After the clothes were rinsed, they had to be put through the wringer to squeeze the water out. I was worn out after all that work, and we were not finished yet. We still had to put the clothes in a basket and hang them on the clothesline to dry. I was too short to reach the line, so my job was to shake out the clothes and hand the clothespins to Mama Lottie.

That was the most work I had ever done in one day. I could hardly wait for dinner. I had worked up a big appetite. Everything went well on our first day, especially considering how much work we did. Finally, it was time for dinner. Rosie and I ate at a small kitchen table by ourselves. She had prepared spaghetti and meatballs. She said Papa Lottie and the boys would be joining her later for dinner. I thought that was weird, but I did not ask why they were not eating with us. We continued to work around the house and play in our room. Some days, we would mop the floors on our hands and knees or make homemade soap in the bathroom tub. Rosie and I would take turns stirring the concoction. We used a large wooden paddle. The paddle was just like something you would use to paddle a boat. We continued to make soap for about a week until we eventually had to stop. Mama Lottie said the problem was with the chemicals she used in making the soap and especially the lye that she used. We had blisters on our hands and arms. Even after we stopped making soap, it took about a month for all the blisters to go away, but our hands never did get soft again. It left our hands dry, like an old lady's.

CHAPTER 13

. . . .

Mystery Girl

After living there for a couple of months, Rosie and I were getting used to our new home. I was still trying to get a glimpse of the little girl in the room across from us. I had seen them take food in her room every day and come out with an empty plate. I was determined to see the little girl even if I had to sneak around to see her. One day, I saw Papa Lottie going into the little girl's room. I heard her talking, and Papa Lottie had left the door cracked. I ran and peeped in the door. I saw a little mixed girl. I could only see the side of her face. Her hair was like a white girl, and her skin was light brown. She looked like she was mixed with both Black and White. Her bed looked huge. It was definitely bigger than my bed. It was sitting in the middle of the room with no windows. She was barely sitting up in that big old bed. I wondered why a little girl like that was in such a big bed. As I was thinking about that big bed, Papa Lottie turned and saw me peeking through the door. He yelled out, "Get away from the door right now!" He scared me so bad. Papa Lottie rarely had two words to say to me. So it really caught me by surprise to hear him speak in such a firm voice directed at me. I quickly ran back into my bedroom and shut the door. I remembered what Mama Lottie said about obeying the rules. I did not want to get a whipping or get put on punishment, so I did not try to look in the little girl's room anymore, and she never came out of her room.

CHAPTER 14

. . . .

Time for School

Summer was ending, and it was almost time for me and Rosie to get registered for school. I was excited to go to school and have the opportunity to be in kindergarten with the other children. Once I got enrolled in school, I really liked my teacher and my classmates. My favorite thing to do was to draw in color with crayons. I was so excited about my newfound passion; I loved coloring anything with Crayolas. I loved the colors of the crayons so much. I started taking the crayons home with me after school. I would put them in a box under my bed, and whenever I had trouble sleeping, I would color something until I fell asleep. After a few weeks of taking the crayons, I had a full box under my bed. Then one day, I was at school, and my teacher announced there would be no more coloring class because most of the crayons had come up missing. She said we would not continue with the art class until all the crayons were returned.

I felt bad, on one hand, that I was holding up the class from having art classes. But on the other hand, I felt good that I had all the crayons under my bed, as if the crayons were keeping me safe or something. I showed my collection of crayons to Rosie and told her what my teacher said about the missing crayons. Rosie was always honest and upright. I should have known not to tell her about my crayons that I hid under the bed. Rosie went straight to Mama Lottie and told her what I had done. Mama Lottie scolded me and told me that was stealing, and we did not have thieves in our house, and

I needed to apologize to my teacher and return all the crayons. As embarrassed as I was for what I had done, I followed Mama Lottie's advice and went to my teacher. I explained to her how I took the crayons day after day until I almost had them all. I also told my teacher how the crayons made me feel safe and helped me to sleep at night. My teacher was very understanding and forgiving. She let me knew, as long as it did not happen again, she had no problem with me. My teacher was a white lady, and that was the first time I had done something wrong and was forgiven right there on the spot. That made me want to be the best crayon-coloring student in the class so I could make my teacher proud of what she taught me.

CHAPTER 15

. . . .

Jack the Bully

We continued to help around the house on weekends. We would wash clothes every weekend until I almost got my hand caught in the washing-machine wringer. Mama Lottie said I was more work than help when it came to washing clothes. After that, every time Mama Lottie washed clothes, she sent me outside. There was nothing in the yard for me to play with. There was only one large tree stump in the center of the yard. The stump looked like someone had been chopping wood on it. There was an axe next to the stump on the ground and a few pieces of wood. While I was standing around trying to find something to do, the older son, named Jack, came up to me and started talking. I was extremely interested in what he had to say since he and his brother hardly spoke a word to me or Rosie. I thought, "Let me pay close attention." I thought this was an opportunity to possibly make him my friend. Then I would have the brother I had always wanted. I had imagined he could protect and teach me things that big brothers taught their little sisters. Instead, I was about to find out that Jack was far from being a protector. He was more like a big bully. After continuously trying to talk to mean-spirited Jack, I gave up and went back in the house for the rest of the day until it was time to go to bed.

The next day, I awoke after getting another good night sleep in my big, cozy bed. I got dressed, ate breakfast, and completed my chores. Then I was ready to attempt playing outside again. I was prepared for Jack by putting my guards up. My plan was not to speak a word to him and keep my distance. I peeked my head out the back door, checking to make sure Jack was not already outside. The back-yard was clear. I proceeded into the middle of the yard. I brought my doll along to keep me company. Just as I got comfortable sitting on the ground with my doll, Jack busted out the door running and yell-ing as he approached me. He yelled, "I see you have not had enough yet! You're back in my yard."

I explained, "Mama Lottie said the backyard was for everyone."

He walked up to me with an angry and commanding voice, grabbed me by my arm, and spoke, "Look up at the sun."

I said, "What?" I thought, *What is he talking about?*

He repeated, "Look at the sun." He started yelling and scream-ing at me and raising his hand as if he were, going to hit me. I began looking around for Rosie or Mama Lottie. I was hoping someone would hear him yelling at me. He said, "If you do not follow my directions, I am going to hurt you." He said again, "Look at the sun and do not make me tell you again."

I tried to follow his directions and look at the sun. It hurt my eyes so bad. I tried turning my face to the sun with my eyes closed, hoping he would be satisfied with my efforts and turn me loose. That just infuriated him more. Suddenly, he grabbed me by the neck and started forcing my head and turning my face toward the sun. I screamed for Rosie to come and help me, but she still could not hear me. He had me in a headlock under his arm, where I could not get loose. Jack then started trying to raise my eyelids with his fingers. He was determined to make me look at the sun. By now my eyes were burning, my nose running, and my face was covered in tears. No matter how I struggled, begged, or tried to look at the sun, Jack would not stop or turn me loose. He said, "I am telling you for the last time, look at the sun," as he was twisting my neck. I tried one more time to look, but I could not. It was painfully blinding. I con-tinued screaming for Mama Lottie and screaming for him to turn me loose.

Mama Lottie finally heard my screams. She came running out the back door approaching us in a fast jogging motion. She slapped

Jack on the back of his head and said, "Boy, leave this girl alone. Go back down in the basement right now." Mama Lottie did not put Jack on punishment. She did nothing to him for abusing me. Instead, she suggested that I stay out of his way, that I should start helping inside the house again and stay from outside as much as possible. I took Mama Lottie's advice and started doing more chores in the house. I would wash, dry, and put away dishes, scrub the floor on my hands and knees, and do many other chores. It only took a couple weeks before I was tired of staying in the house with Mama Lottie. She was working me like a slave. After about a month constantly working with Mama Lottie, I could not take it any longer. I tried to get Rosie to go outside with me, but Rosie liked staying in the house all the time. Unlike me, I loved the outdoors. I eventually decided to take my chances and venture back outside. I had found a small plastic ball in the corner of the yard next to the fence. But it was only a few days later when Jack the bully had returned. When Jack saw me playing with the ball, he took the ball from me. He started throwing the ball at me and hitting me with the ball. I said to myself, "Let me hurry up and go back in the house."

CHAPTER 16

. . . .

Sucking My Thumb

I stuck my thumb in my mouth and walked away. Sucking my thumb was a bad habit I had. I occasionally sucked my thumb whenever I was nervous or afraid. Mama Lottie had scolded me about sucking my thumb when we first moved there. She said sucking my thumb had to come to an end. Well, evidently, Jack overheard the conversation concerning sucking my thumb. So when he saw me put my thumb in my mouth, he was more than happy to remind me of what his mom had said. Jack began to bully me and threaten to cut off my thumb. He yelled at me, saying, "My mother warned you about sucking your thumb." I could see in his eyes he was thinking something bad. I started crying and tried to make a run for the house, but he reached out real fast and grabbed me by the arm. He said in a wicked voice, "Now I am going to cut off your thumb." He looked over at the tree stump and saw the axe lying on the ground. He yanked me by the arm and pulled me over to the tree stump. Forcing my head between his thighs while choking me, Jack was using one hand to hold my arm on the stump. He bent down and struggled to pick up the heavy axe with his other hand.

At that time, I knew I better get myself free or I was going to lose a thumb. I tried with all my might to free myself. That just fueled his fire more, and he tightened the grip he had on my head until I felt like I was becoming unconscious. As he continued to raise the axe, he forced my little hand down on the tree stump, positioning it to chop it off. Just as he was beginning to execute the swinging motion down onto my poor little thumb, Mama Lottie screamed out at the top of her voice, "Put that axe down, Jack! Drop that axe right now!" He stopped in the middle of his swing. The axe was still in the air. He just dropped the axe right there on the ground. I fell to my knees on the ground. He scared me so bad I could not stand up. Mama Lottie ran to me and picked me up and carried me into the house. She told Jack to go back in the basement and stay there until she told him to come out. She continued to tell him that he was on punishment. She said, "I have told you too many times already to leave these little girls alone."

After that day, things seemed to calm down for a few months. I could go outside and play without being harassed or threatened by Jack. Todd never said anything to me or Rosie. He just looked at us like we were dirt. I did not see her sons much after that incident. They basically stayed in the basement, and when we ate dinner or breakfast, they continued to eat at different times than me and Rosie. The little girl was still in her room. I still had not seen her face totally, but I continued to hear her voice when they would go in her room.

CHAPTER 17

. . . .

Branded

As things improved around the house, Rosie and I continued to excel in school, enjoying the whole learning process. Using my crayons was still my passion as I would try to perfect every little line that I put onto the paper. Days and weeks continued to pass. Then one day, Mama Lottie got a letter in the mail from the state of Colorado. The letter was informing Mamma Lottie that Rosie and I needed to take some kind of test or some kind of shot. She said the information on the letter was somewhat confusing, but we still had to go. The letter was informing us that an appointment day and time had already been set up. The letter stated that we were to be at the neighborhood clinic the next week in the afternoon. I was not too concerned. I had gotten plenty of shots. Rosie and I were pretty tough little girls when it came to getting shots. On the day of our appointment, Mama Lottie drove us to the clinic. It seemed like we got there so fast. The clinic was a one-story brick building. As soon as we walked in the door, we saw several children crying. When I saw that, I should have known then that it must be more than a shot. The kids would go in the room fine and come out looking like they had been tortured. I had never seen kids looked like that from just getting a shot.

I guess Mama Lottie noticed the same thing and asked the nurse, "What kind of shots are they giving?"

The nurse answered and said, "Oh! They're not here to get shots. The reason you and everyone else here received a letter is because your foster children are the property of the state of Colorado, and your children do not have any visible birthmarks on their bodies." She went on to say, "Due to so many children being lost or, worse, in the foster care system, the state of Colorado mandated that all foster-care children have some kind of identifiable mark on them. And if they do not have a birthmark or some kind of identifying scar, the doctor will have to put one on them. The state is paying for it all. There is absolutely no cost to you. It is a simple process. Each child will be getting a cut or scrape on them. It will be on their backs for identification purposes only." And then she said, "It only takes a few minutes once you are inside the room with the doctor. After the procedure, the doctor will be giving you some medicine to take home to put on the mark. The medicine will keep it from getting infected. After the procedure is over, the doctor will record the precise location of the mark on their bodies and add it into their medical records." The nurse asked if Mama Lottie had any other questions, and she answered no.

When the nurse called my name, she had a chart in her hand. She instructed me to follow her. They took Rosie and I into separate examining rooms. Mama Lottie was trying to follow behind me into the room, but the nurse stopped her. She told her that no parents were allowed in the examination rooms with the doctor. I continued on into the doctor's examination room. The doctor was sitting on a stool with some kind of knife in his hand. He was signaling for me to come closer. As I got closer, the nurse lifted the back of my shirt. As soon as I was close enough for the doctor to reach out to me, he said, "Do not be afraid. This will only take a moment." Then he reached out and pulled me by my arm closer to him. He turned me around with my back facing him. He took what I thought was a knife, but actually, it was a straight razor. When he ran that razor blade across my back, I screamed. The doctor just handed the nurse some medicine and said, "Give this to her mom and get the next child, please." The doctor did not look at me. He just signaled for me to leave the room by pointing his finger and telling me to follow the nurse. The nurse took me by the hand and led me back to the waiting room.

I was crying, my nose was running, and my back was hurting and burning.

Mama Lottie was still sitting and waiting patiently in the waiting room. As the nurse walked me back to the waiting room, the nurse gave Mama Lottie a jar of something that looked like grease and a bottle of red iodine. She explained the doctor's instructions to Mama Lottie, then we went home. It took about two weeks for our cuts to heal. Eventually, Rosie and I both were able to have our bandages removed. I felt like I had been branded like an animal. Rosie and I had both got our marks on the lower right side of our backs. Our marks healed, and we continued with our lives as normal children.

CHAPTER 18

. . . .

Christmas Time

The weather had changed and gotten colder, but Rosie and I were excited because Christmas time was coming. It was in the month of December when Mama Lottie informed us that we were invited to go to the toy drive for foster children. She explained how a school bus would be picking me and Rosie up. She said the bus would take us to a warehouse where the toys would be distributed. After a couple of weeks passed, the school bus came, just like Mama Lottie said. Rosie and I were so happy. I felt like finally something good was coming out of being a foster child. We boarded a big yellow bus that was already full of other children. The ride was about twenty minutes long. On our way, all the children were laughing and talking to one another, having a good time. When we arrived, there were a couple of other buses with children already there unloading and forming a line leading into the building. We waited for a while, and it was finally our time to get off the bus and get in line.

I was so excited! I was hoping for a bike with some training wheels on it, but I was grateful to get whatever they gave me. When we walked in the building, all I could see was Santa Clause sitting up high on some kind of platform. There were children already in line walking up to Santa. He was giving them a Christmas gift. I looked, but I did not see any bikes anywhere. When my turn came, I walked up to Santa and looked him in his eyes. He asked me my name. Then he said he had a couple of special gifts for me. He reached to the side of his chair and picked up two boxes and handed them to me. and said, "Merry Christmas." Rosie and I returned home with two new dolls each. I did not get a bike, but I still loved my dolls. Rosie and I stayed up late into the night, talking about our trip on the bus and seeing Santa. We played with our dolls in the bedroom until we fell asleep.

I was awakened to the sounds of walkie-talkies. There were the sound of police radios right outside our room in the hallway. Rosie was asleep, so I thought maybe I was dreaming. I listened closely to make sure I was not dreaming. Once I heard a white man's voice, asking "Where did the little girl get the pills from?" I sat straight up in the bed and woke Rosie up. We got out of bed and cracked the door open and peeped through the crack. We could see paramedics and police going in and out of the little girl's bedroom. She was being rolled out on a stretcher. I heard a policeman asking Mama Lottie more questions about the girl. He mentioned something again about pills and where she got them from. Then the officer noticed me and Rosie peeking through the door.

He walked over to our door, looked down at us, and said, "Hello, girls," then he turned to Mama Lottie and asked her how many more children were in this house.

She replied, "Other than my two sons, just these two."

The officer pushed the door open and said to me and Rosie, "Girls, you need to get dressed because you will be leaving this house shortly, and you will not be returning."

They did not tell us what was wrong with the little girl or how she got sick. I wondered why they covered her head up when that would make it hard for her to breathe. Plus, I was still trying to see her face. Mama Lottie walked over to us along with a police lady by her side. She had tears in her eyes, and her voice was cracking as she said, "Girls, I am so sorry, I am so sorry. I hope you find another good home. But for now, you have to get all of your belongings because the social worker is on her way, and you need to be ready when she gets here." And then she said, "I love you, girls. Both of you are good girls." She turned, and the police walked her out the door.

Our social worker arrived and tried to explain to us that the little girl had had an accident, but that was all she knew, and there was nothing else that she could tell us. And because of that accident, Mama Lottie and Papa Lottie could not have foster kids in their home anymore. The social worker said, "That is why you girls are going back to your grandmother's until we can find you another foster home."

CHAPTER 19

. . . .

A New School with New Opportunities

Our grandmother enrolled us in a school as soon as we got back to her house. I think she planned for us to be with her for a while. The school was quite a distance from their home. It was larger than this school I had just left with Mama Lottie. This school had a lot to offer. It had all kinds of programs that you could participate in, like plays, singing, acting, and dancing. I was mostly interested in acting. There was a play they were just getting ready to launch called *Snow White*. The teacher asked the class, "Does anyone want to play the role of Snow White?" My hand went straight up. I did not give any thought to the color of my skin, although I was the only Black student in the class. So I expected to get the role of Snow White, just like anybody else. Except when my teacher saw my hand up, she volunteered me for the part of the wicked witch. I was not interested in being a wicked witch. I was a nice little girl, and I wanted to be Snow White. But my teacher asked the class, "How many of you think Elaine would make a good wicked witch? Raise your hands." They all laughed and raised their hands.

I said to myself, "I am new to this school, and they do not even know me. What makes them so sure I will be a good wicked witch?" I did not think that my color had anything to do with it. Being the happy child that I was, I gladly took the role of the wicked witch to ensure that I would be able to participate in the play. I practiced my lines every day, saying "Who is the fairest of them all?" On the day of the play, I played my part to the best of my ability, and my grandmother and grandfather came to see me perform. At the end of the show, they clapped and stood up, as if I was a great actor. I said to myself, "This is what I want to do. I have found my new passion."

I really liked my school and the children in the school, but I could not say the same for my teacher. She was not like my teacher when I lived with Mama Lottie. She would always cut me off when I would be trying to say something, or if I raised my hand in class, she would not call on me. If I had to go to the restroom, she would always tell me I had to wait, but I noticed she did not tell everybody they had to hold it or wait. One day, I had to go really bad to the restroom. I approached her desk and told her I needed to be excused to go to the restroom. She told me to take my seat and I had to wait until class was over. I took my seat, and I tried my best to hold it, but once one drop came, it continued to flow. My chair was at the back of the class, so she could not see the puddle that had made its way to the floor. I just moved my skirt out the way to make sure it would not get wet. I did not know what else to do. I could not hold it any longer. I asked her to let me go to the restroom, but she would not. I had no other choice but to pee right there. When it was time to go home, I got up with the rest of the children, went outside, and lined up and got on the bus.

Later that day, my grandmother got a call from the school, saying the teacher had reported me peeing in my chair in class. My grandmother was a proud woman. Peeing in the chair in the class was something that she did not expect to happen with her grandchildren. But my grandmother was also a loving, understanding woman and did not judge me before asking me what happened. When I explained to my grandmother how I had asked repeatedly to go to the restroom and my teacher continued to deny me, my grandmother said she was going to have a talk with the principal and for me to not worry because she knew me well enough to know that was something I would not have done unless I had no other choice. That was why I loved my grandmother so much. She was a wise woman. But that did not keep me from having to go back to school again, and it was hard facing those children after my teacher told them all I peed in the chair, and they laughed at me. That made all the children want to distance themselves from me, like I was dirty. That feeling that I got in the classroom the first day I returned, it was an overwhelming sense of shame even though I knew I could not help it. I told myself I never wanted to show my face in that school again.

The next day, I told my grandmother that I had missed the bus and the bus driver did not see me or he didn't stop. I told the lie so I could stay home that day. I told her the same story for about three days in a row. On the fourth day, she realized I was missing the bus on purpose, so she walked me to the bus stop and made sure I got on the bus. The next day, in the nick of time, my grandmother got a call from our social worker. She said my mom was being released from the hospital in two weeks, and she would be able to take possession of all her children. We were all scattered throughout the city of Denver in different foster homes. Seeing my sisters and my mother again was going to be wonderful. The next day, the social worker showed up at my grandparents' house to let me and Rosie know that our mother was being released from the hospital again and to confirm that we would be leaving our grandmother's in a couple of weeks. She said the doctors had put my mom on some type of medication, and they recommended that getting her children back would help her to recover faster. It seemed like that two weeks took forever. Because I was still going to the school that I had been put to shame, I still hung in there anyway and did my best to learn.

CHAPTER 20

. . . .

Returning Home with Mom

Finally, moving day had come, and we were moving back into the same project that we were living in before. There were a lot of people that gave my mother donations. Some were large items like furniture and a few small items like a toaster and a radio. All this was to make her feel better and help her get reestablished. Because when she returned home, my mom was a lot better physically and mentally, she was singing again and whistling with her beautiful voice. A few of her favorite songs were by Nat King Cole, Jackie Wilson, and The Platters. She had started cooking breakfast and dinner again. She was having conversations with us about our schools and showing a genuine interest in our daily lives. It was great having my mother back.

On the first of the month, the government disbursed boxes of food and blankets to the needy. They called the boxes commodities. My mom said the commodities would normally be given to US soldiers. She said since there was no war, the soldiers did not need it. I asked my mom if I could use the cups to make mud pies and the blankets to make tents in the yard. The commodities box also had butter, cheese, peanut butter, powdered milk, canned meat, and other foods. My mother learned how to cook everything with the powdered milk and powdered eggs. I could eat almost anything but not her powdered eggs. She just did not know how to cook them.

Mama was doing so well. She had started meeting other people. On occasion, a male friend would stop by the house to visit with her. The problem was, my mom fell in love with every man that she brought home. And before we knew it, she would start talking about having that baby boy.

CHAPTER 21

. . . .

The Father I Wished I Had

My mother started dating Mr. Ted. He was a polite and intelligent man. I remembered him taking me and my mom to the Denver Art Museum of History. It was an awesome experience. There were giant dinosaur fossils and skeletons. There were all kinds of animals behind glass display models. They looked so real, like they could come out of the glass. You could push a button at the bottom of the glass, and a recording would come on and tell you all about the history of that animal. While strolling past one of the display windows, we got to a display that I could barely see because it was above my head. My mom saw something in that display that she liked, and I wanted to see it also. I was standing on my tippy toes trying to see in the glass when Mr. Ted reached down and picked me up. Then he leaned over the glass so I could get a good look at the miniature Indian village. The fact that Mr. Ted cared enough to pick me up so I could see in the glass made me wish he was my dad. Mr. Ted continued to carry me throughout the entire exhibit and through the museum.

At the end of our visit, Mr. Ted took us out to eat at a restaurant. It was called McDonalds. It was the first time I had eaten in a restaurant. We each had a hamburger, fries, and a pop. I had the time of my life with Momma and Ted. I wanted Mr. Ted to be my dad so bad. I wished we could be a normal family that took trips together and did other things that families did. But unfortunately, by the time I got comfortable with Mr. Ted being around the house, their relationship was coming to an end. My hopes for a family had again been suddenly crushed. My mom told me that she and Mr. Ted were no longer seeing each other and to stop asking her about his return because he was gone and would not be returning.

CHAPTER 22

. . . .

A Different Kind of Church

My mother started taking us to church, but it did not look like church because the church was in the pastor's front room of his house. There were four rows of chairs and a long table and a chair at the front of the room. The walls were all painted bright white, and there were no windows. The pastor's name was Rev. Reese. He was an average, medium-built older Black man. He was soft spoken and appeared to be very kind. Rev. Reese had a car. He would make two trips to the projects, one trip to pick up me, my mother, my sisters and a second trip to pick up as many children that would fit in his car. All my sisters hated going to his church. It's because the service was so long. I was thrilled to go because he served Sunday dinner following services. I was not about to miss a free meal no matter how long I had to wait.

My mother and Rev. Reese begun dating. That meant Rev. Reese was spending a lot of time at our house for one reason or another. He also had a part-time job as a custodian at a local bakery. When Rev. Reese finished his shift at work, he would bring us the pies that were rejected during the cooking process. The bakers would toss all the reject pies into a box that sat outside the back door of the store. Sometimes the box would flip over, and the pies would fall on the ground. Rev. Reese would just scoop them up and put them right back in the box. I found this out when I asked Rev. Reese why some pies had rocks and others did not. He was happy to explain and laughing, saying, "He who eats the most pies eats the most rocks." And he continued to laugh. The pies I ate were full of pieces of rocks and some leaves, especially the pies that were at the bottom of the box. I learned how to separate the rocks and leaves by the time he arrived the next week with a second box. I enjoyed all the varieties of pies. There were lemon meringue, cherry, blueberry, apple, and some cream-filled pies. They were all so good. I just had to take my time and make sure they were not gritty.

My mother stopped going to church for whatever reason. After that, Rev. Reese started spending nights at our house on a regular basis. I still wanted to go to church even if my mom did not. So the next Sunday, Rev. Reese continued to take me and a couple of the neighborhood girls to church. We would sit in church and listen to Rev. Reese while falling asleep in our chairs, then awaking to him still speaking, saying a bunch of words we did not understand. It did not seem to matter if we were paying him any attention or not just as long as we stayed in our seats. We continued going to church week after week for a few months. Rev. Reese always cooked the best biscuits and fried chicken after each service. I loved the smell of chicken when it was frying. We had butter and syrup for our biscuits. Nothing was going to keep me from going to church and getting a meal like that every Sunday. That was all I thought about all week.

Things seemed to be going great. Rev. Rees said that me and the two other little girls from the neighborhood (Lilly and Maggy) were his favorite church members. He had stopped picking up the other children. One Sunday, Rev. Rees asked me, Lilly, and Maggy if we would like to have some real fun after church. We excitedly answered, "Yes, we would!"

He said, "Okay, then go hop in the car and let us all go for a ride."

As we were riding, he repeated a couple of times, "Are you girls willing to do whatever you're told to do? Because if you are, I will give you $5 each." We started hopping up and down in the car. We were ecstatic and kept repeating in saying yes, definitely yes. He continued driving to an isolated location. Then as we got closer, it looked to be an abandoned junkyard. Rev. Reese parked the car and said,

"We're going to play a little game. But first, I have to ask you girls a question. Have any of you girls started menstruating?" We were so young and naive. We did not even know what menstruation was. We had no clue what he was talking about. Then he said, "You know, your period." We were still clueless. I guess he was pleased with our ignorance and assumed that we evidently had not started our period. Then he asked who wanted to be first to get their $5. I raised my hand faster than everyone else. We began to argue with one another. We were all eager to be the first to get our $5. I said if it were not for me, they would not even know Rev. Reese, so I should be the first to get the $5. They agreed and told me, "Okay, go ahead."

Rev. Reese said, "Now that we know who is first. Elaine, you need to climb over the seat and get up here with me in the front seat."

Once I got comfortable sitting in the front seat, he told me and the other girls to take off our underwear. In the back seat, the girls' eyes were getting bigger and bigger as they were looking on, wondering what was getting ready to happen. I had no idea what he was planning to do. First, he told me to lie down. Then he tried to lie on top of me, but he was too heavy. I could not breathe. Then he worked his way to the side and tried to insert his private part in my private part. I yelled, "Stop, that hurts!" He tried to continue, then I said, "No, you are trying to hurt me." And I pushed him off me. I hopped back into the back seat with the girls, saying repeatedly, "No, he is trying to hurt us. This is not a game we want to play, and he needs to take us home."

He saw the look on my face, and he must have gotten afraid. He started yelling, "Okay, okay, you do not have to do anything. Just promise me you will not tell anybody. If you all promise not to ever tell what just happened, I will still give you the $5 anyway."

I thought that was fair enough if we did not have to do anything else and still got our $5. I talked to the girls, and we all agreed we would keep our mouths shut. He gave each of us our $5 and kept his word and did not touch us. He took us back to the projects and dropped us off like nothing ever happened. That was our last time playing games or going to church with Rev. Reese. The girls and I never mentioned what happened on that day to our parents or anyone else.

I noticed my mom's stomach getting bigger after a few months. I asked my mom if she was pregnant, and she said yes, and she was hoping for a boy. I thought it would be nice not to be the baby in the house, and it would give me someone to play with and take care of. The nine months my mom was pregnant went by so fast. Before I knew it, my mom was going to the hospital to deliver the baby. I was all excited that I was about to be the big sister to the baby. After a few days at the hospital, my mom returned home with no baby. I was devastated and inquired, "Where is the baby?"

My mom simply said, "They said I have enough children to care for, and I had to leave that baby at the hospital." I was so sad I did not know what to do. I had never heard that a family had to leave their babies at the hospital because they could not take care of them. I kept asking questions until my mom yelled at me to stop asking so many questions. Then she said it was another girl.

Within the next couple of months, my mom had found herself a new boyfriend to keep her entertained, but my mom was still obsessed with the ideal of having a baby boy. She felt her whole life would be better if she had a son. She talked about wanting a son to me and my sisters day and night. My sisters and I also wanted a brother. And if a boy would help my mom be a better person, I was all for a baby brother. I grew up thinking that boys and men were superior to girls and women. I developed that way of thinking by the way my mother talked about having a baby boy. She was constantly saying if she only had a boy, she would be happy. I tried so hard to make her happy, but she would go right back to wishing for a boy. That made me have a curiosity about boys. Why did my mom like boys better than the five girls she already had? I constantly wondered what boys smelled like or why they peed standing up. As a child, I had all kinds of questions like that, but I dared not to let my mom know or any other adult know about my curiosity. I would have been labeled as a bad child for thinking such thoughts, so I kept my thoughts to myself.

After that incident with Rev. Reese, I became very observative of people and especially adults. I tried to listen to their hearts and not their mouths. Being around Rev. Reese for so many months taught me several valuable lessons. It was like I had a wake-up call to reality. I finally understood what my old friend Shirley Pittman and her mom meant when they called my mom all those names. They knew what kind of men my mom was sleeping with. I was forced to admit the truth about my mom. She really did sleep with all kinds of men. I began to wonder after Rev. Reese tried to molest me, and I did not tell my mom. I asked myself, "What about my older sisters? Had they been assaulted, molested?" Or like in my case, I had experienced an attempt of molestation. At that point, I said, "I do not want to grow up and be like my mom." I made a promise to myself right then. I said, "When I grow up, I will get married, and the only man that will be around my children will be their father." When I thought more about Rev. Reese, I considered him the worst of all my mom's boyfriends because he used the Bible, fried chicken, and biscuits to win my trust. His Bible looked just like my grandmother's Bible. And I had previously shared with him how I loved my grandmother to read Bible stories to me. He took everything I told him and tried to use it for his own lustful purpose.

Needless to say, Rev. Reese removed all his things from our house on the same day he paid us the $5. As a matter of fact, it was like Rev. Reese disappeared from the face of the earth after that day. My mom never spoke of him, and I never told her what he attempted to do. Meanwhile, within the next couple of months, my mom had found herself a new boyfriend. Money was still tight and getting tighter. I was glad that Rev. Reese was gone, but I had to admit, I missed the Sunday fried-chicken meals and the boxes full of pies. By the end of the month, I was back looking for my next meal. It seemed like the food commodities got less and less each month. It was not long before I found myself back to searching for food in the trash cans all over again.

CHAPTER 23

. . . .

The Initiation into the Club

One day, while searching through the trash cans, a group of kids approached me. They said they had noticed me going from one trash can to another. Then one of them stepped forward and said his name was Henry. He went on to introduce the rest of the group, saying, "This is little James, Larry, Chuck, and Donna." Henry looked to be about fourteen years of age, dark-skinned, and skinny. The other children looked to be about nine, ten, and eleven years old. They were all older than me. Donna and Chuck looked like they could have been sister and brother, but they were not. They were both light-skinned with jet-black hair. Little James was also light-skinned with light-green eyes. He was kind of cute. Henry went on talking about all the benefits that came with being a club member, like not having to dig in trash cans looking for food anymore. And if anyone dared to bother me, they would fight my battle. He said, "Once we accept you as a member, you have to become a blood brother or sister. You just have to choose one of us for the initiation ritual."

I said, "I choose little James."

Henry said, "When you carve your initials, there will be enough blood for us to tie your wrist together with your brother. After that, we initiate you into the club."

That did not sound bad, considering the benefits I would get in exchange—food, protection, no more fighting off dogs in the trash cans and friends also. It sounded good to me. I yelled out, "Yes, I want to be a member! When can I sign up?"

Henry turned and consulted with the other children for a few minutes, and then he replied, saying, "The following Saturday would be a good day. But first, we need to go to your house to see where you live."

I said, "Oh no, my mother is not going to want to meet you all."

He replied, "Do not worry, we do not want to meet your mother or any of your family members."

I thought, *Great,* because they would ruin this great opportunity that I now had to become a member.

Henry told me to show them where I lived. I was more than happy to show them. I took them straight to my house and pointed it out to them. One more thing, Henry said in a firm voice, "When you are with the members, do not tell anyone where you are going or why you are going with us."

I agreed, and they said their goodbyes and left.

That following Saturday, little James did exactly what he was told. He met me at the corner of my housing project, ready and eager to take me to the clubhouse. We walked for about seven or eight blocks until we reached a wide-open dirt field. I could see the members of the club. They were standing by a big tree in the distance. I was observing everything around me as we approached the members. The first thing I noticed was a big hole in the ground. It looked like a cave close to the tree. The hole was big enough for two people to fit in. Little James said, "Elaine, I hope you remember the route we took to get here. And remember the big tree in the middle of the field because it is the landmark to find the cave. The next time we meet here, you will have to find it by yourself."

As Little James was talking and we were all saying our hellos, Henry emerged from the dugout in the ground. He said, "I am glad you made it, Elaine. So let us go inside the cave and get you initiated. Everything is ready." One look at the cave opening and I was hesitant to go inside it. Henry could see the look of fear on my face. So Henry yelled out, "There is nothing to be afraid of! Just follow me." He went in the opening headfirst and yelled to me, "Come on!"

I stuck my head in and then my body. We were crawling on our hands and knees until we reached a large opening at the end of the cave. This portion of the cave had been carved out nicely. The walls and ceilings were supported by cardboard and wooden sticks for extra support. We also had a big piece of cardboard to each sit on. I was surprised how much room there was once we got inside. There were two candles burning in the middle of the cave. It was damp and still rather dark. Little James and I were given a flashlight each. That was to help us to see each other clearer. Henry said, "Now that you have chosen little James as your blood brother, it is time for you to carve his initials into your wrist."

We were all sitting in a circle with our legs folded. As I took the razor blade from Henry's hand, the members sat quietly with anticipation on their faces, and one of them said, "It's time. Go ahead."

I started carving into my left wrist slowly and lightly. I had begun shaking as I saw a little blood emerge. It started hurting, so I tried not to cut past the top layer of skin. Little James was sitting next to me. He was carving my initials into his wrist and smiling at me at the same time. I continued carving until the L and J was complete. I wanted to complain and say how bad my wrist was hurting, but I wanted to seem tough. I dared not to show pain or any more fear in front of them. As soon as our initials were completely carved into our wrists, Henry shouted, "Yes, it has been done!" He wrapped our wrists together with a thin white cloth. Then he continued securing our wrists together using a rope. When he was finished, he sat up on his knees. He reached out and grabbed our arms, then lifted them up in the air. He said a few words, which I did not understand, like he was performing some kind of ritual. After that, he said, "Elaine, you are now an official member of our club."

. . . .

CHAPTER 24

Report and Be Ready for Work

Henry asked me, "Are you ready for your first assignment?"

I eagerly said, "Yes!"

He said, "Then report with the group on the front lawn of Laradon Hall on the next day."

I replied, "I know exactly where you are talking about, and I will be there."

Henry informed us that we would be picking apples and plums on this particular job. He said that he had already scouted out an area that had an abundance of fruit trees. The plan was for us to start at night while everyone was asleep. He explained that the big boys would cut off the large branches from the trees. The smaller or shorter kids' assignment was to climb the trees and shake off the fruit. My job was to gather the fruit off the ground and put it in the pillowcases Henry gave me. After receiving our instructions, we all retired to our homes to get a good night's sleep.

The next day, everyone showed up on the lawn about eight at night. All five of us were ready to go with our pillowcases, cutting saws, ropes, and whatever else Henry thought we needed to get the job done. He said our tree-cutting job was located about a mile away. We picked up our things at Laradon Hall and headed down the dark, quiet streets. There was just the sounds of dogs barking on and off. When we reached the designated area, Henry spoke in a soft, low voice and pointed to each tree we were to remove the fruit and branches. Once we gathered and secured the fruit in the pillowcases, our job was done. The bigger boys were busy trying to tie the large branches together using a rope. Once the rope was secured to the ends of the branches, a couple of boys pulled the other end of the ropes and dragged the branches all the way back to the projects. We all gathered back on the lawn of the Hall. Henry proudly stood in front of us and announced that we had successfully carried out our mission by obtaining our food for the week. I was surprised how well his plan worked and how well the group worked together.

. . . .

CHAPTER 25

Riding the Train to Work

The next week, Henry had another job for us in the daytime. It required us to hop on and ride a freight train or a boxcar into town. I was afraid to ride the train, but I had to do what they said if I wanted to stay in the club. So I got over my fear and hopped on the train with everyone else when it was time. The train would shake violently when it would start to move and shake again violently when it picked up speed. Then we reached our destination at the train yard. The train yard was where all the trains would go to pick up or deliver their goods. Henry would walk up and down the courtyard, closely considering if a boxcar had food in it and deciding the best boxcar to open. When he finished looking, Henry conceded he had no idea what was in any of those boxes. He said the boxcars were marked differently from his last visit. So he said he would just have to take a chance and surprise us all.

Henry opened the first boxcar with a crowbar and a hammer. The boxcar door was made of steal and was hard to slide open. We all put our hands on the door and pushed until it slid open. To our surprise, the boxcar was full of watermelons. Henry and a couple of the guys pulled three watermelons out of the boxcar. I said, "How are we going to open them? We do not have a knife."

Henry said just watch this, then he thrashed the watermelon onto the ground and cracked it open. He asked me if I still needed a knife. I said no, and he replied, "Well, grab a piece." He continued to crack open the other watermelons. We all sat down right there in the train yard and ate until we got our fill of the three watermelons. The watermelons were delicious, but they presented a problem trying to carry them back to the projects. So Henry opened a second boxcar using the same crowbar and hammer. This boxcar was full of bags of frozen strawberries. Henry said, "They may not taste as good as the watermelons, but they will be a lot easier to carry." We loaded up our pillowcases to the top with the bags of strawberries.

When I got home with all my strawberries, I put them in the refrigerator. My mom asked me where I got all those strawberries from. I told her that a boy named Henry, his friends, and I got them off a train. Her response was, "Well, will you ask Henry if he could get some peaches off the train?"

I replied, "Yes, ma'am, I will get you some peaches next time."

For the next couple of months, we continued to work locally, dragging fruit back to the projects and cutting down tree limbs. Sometimes the homeowners made it easy for us because they knew we were hungry and understood why we were ravishing their fruit trees, but some homeowners were not as nice. As a matter of fact, they would try to catch us by coming out their homes and shoot at us as we ran away. Eventually, Henry concluded the risks were not worth getting shot over a basket of fruit. He said it was not making sense anymore.

CHAPTER 26

. . . .

Bigger Jobs, Bigger Pay

Henry thought he would take our jobs to a higher level. When he said that, he really meant it. Our next job consisted of our group traveling about two or three miles on foot. There was a little candy store that Henry had his eyes on for a while. He said this was a sophisticated job because the owners lived on top of the business. He said he knew how to make the job quite simple. Henry shared his plans with the group. We all agreed to meet at the Hall around 10:00 p.m. with pillowcases in hand. I was excited and frightened at the same time. I felt excited that I was going to bring home a pillowcase full of candy. On the other hand, I was scared to death we might get caught.

Our walk started out fine, but after walking for about thirty minutes, I was getting tired. When we reached the bottom of the hill, the street merged into a two-lane busy street, going north and south. Henry yelled out, "Just in case we get separated for any reason! Notice there are two big hills. The one we just came down, and the other one on the left has the big store at the top, named Bomarito's."

Thinking back, I remembered that store. That was the store my sister Raney took me to a while back. Bomarito's was a mom-and-pop store that served hot dogs, hamburgers, and Mexican food. I remembered a really nice white man that owned the store. His name was Mr. Bomarito. He helped me one day when I ordered some extremely hot Mexican food from his lunch counter. He gave me free milk and ice cream to stop my mouth from burning. Mr. Bomarito was so nice. I said, then, I would never forget that store or the owner, Mr. Bomarito. Meanwhile, the members and I had spent almost an hour or more getting to our location. We still had to cross a busy street with traffic going in both directions. It was a lot of traffic; plus, it was dark. We finally reached our destination. Henry yelled out, "Well, there it is!"

I said to myself, "What? That is a house, not a store!" It was a two-story, wood-frame house with a sign on it that read "Candy Store."

We were all huddled together in an old, abandoned building across the street from the store. Henry said he was going to the store to check things out. We were told to stay put until he gave all clear signals. We waited, and then we saw the signal. Off we went running across the busy street and into an open field with tall, overgrown weeds. The field was on the same property as the store. Henry got us in a huddle and told each of us our jobs and positions to take. Then Henry said, "Okay, it's showtime. Follow me." We went to the back of the house. There were a couple of steps leading up to the back door, which had a small glass window in it. Henry had an object in his hand. He said it was a glass cutter. He spoke in a whispering voice. He said, "All I have to do is cut a hole in this glass, stick my hand through, and unlock the door." He was cutting in a circle. As he repeatedly tried to remove the circle of glass, the glass would not give way. So he had to tap on the glass with his tool to get the glass to fall out. Once the door was open. I was instructed to run in first because I was the smallest. We each had an assigned area to get candy. The plan was to grab the candy extremely fast. Fill our pillowcases up and get out as fast as we could. That sound pretty simple when Henry said it.

The problem was, when Henry kept tapping on the glass, the store owner evidently heard him tapping. The sound must have gotten the owner's attention. As I ran deep into the store, I was breathing hard, and my adrenaline was rushing. I could see the candy case, just like Henry described. I opened my pillowcase with one hand and grabbed a fistful of candy with the other hand. There were lollipops, bubblegum, caramel candy, chocolate, and much more. As I went to get a second handful, the owner yelled out, "Who is down there?" The owner heard the commotion we were making with our little hands rambling through the candy. He stood at the top of the stairs for a moment, then peeked his head down and around the corner, and he creeped down a couple of stairs in his bare feet and pajamas. He was moving so slowly to investigate the commotion. I was standing right below the staircase. I was so close I could smell his feet. I was petrified I could not move. Everyone else must have been petrified too because no one was moving. The owner must have seen one of the kids because he yelled out, "What the hell? Let me get my gun. I am going to kill all you bastards!"

Henry yelled out, "Get out! Everybody, come on, get out right now! Run for your lives!"

The owner started cussing and yelling, saying he was going to shoot us all. When he turned to get his gun, everyone ran and made it out of the store but me. They were all closer to the door than I was. By the time I got to the door, the owner was coming back down the stairs with a rifle. I ran out the door and into the backyard. I continued running into the field of overgrown weeds next to the house. I could hear Henry's voice from a distance, saying, "Keep running and stay low." As I was running, I looked back and saw the owner, in his pajamas, shooting into the weeds. He was trying his best to hit someone. He turned and started in my direction, as if he heard me. I had to stop, or he would see the weeds move and know where to shoot. I crunched down low to the ground and prayed, "God, Jesus, please help me." Then I looked around to see if there were any other kids in the field, but they had already gotten away.

He continued walking, cursing, and shooting into the weeds randomly until I could see his feet standing right before me. My heart was racing, but I dared not to move or breathe too hard. He was almost standing over me. I almost peed y pants. He stood there for a few minutes. Then I heard him say, "Damn it, the little suckers got away." Eventually, he gave up and returned to his yard and went back inside his house. I still did not move for about twenty more minutes just in case he was trying to trick me to stand up. When I felt the coast was clear, I crawled on my hands and knees through the field. When I thought it was safe to stand up, I started running. I was mad that my club members had left me. I was trying to remember how to get back home. I had not paid a lot of attention to the direction since Henry led us there. I just knew I was a long way from home, and it was the middle of the night. I remembered what Henry said about the two big hills. There was that store named Bomarito's at the top of one. All I had to do was find the hills. I kept walking in the direction I thought was right. I finally spotted the big hill with the store on top from a distance. Then I saw the other hill that led to my neighborhood. I was so relieved.

After crossing the big street, I was halfway up the hill when I heard a voice shout out, "There's Elaine!"

"That is Elaine! I see her!" one of the voices shouted. I could not see anyone. It was so dark, but it sounded like my club members.

"Where?" asked another voice.

They replied, "Over there. Look, she is coming up the hill."

I looked toward where the voices were coming from, and I could see a group of kids snuggled by a building. They started coming into focus. Then I heard Henry's voice yell out, saying, "That is her, everybody! That is her!" All of a sudden, you could see their faces as they were emerging from their hiding place. They came running and hugged me tight. Henry said, "I hope you know we were not going to leave you there. We were hiding up here, trying to figure out how we could get back down there and help you. We decided that we needed to wait till daylight. I promise you, we were coming back for you."

After my close encounter with death, I told Henry that I did not want to be in the club anymore. He said he understood, but I would always be a friend of the club members. Then Henry said something I did not expect to hear from him. He said honestly he was thinking about breaking up the club and quitting himself. He said he wanted to look for a real job with real pay. So we all gave one another a hug and said our goodbyes. I still had my pillowcase with my handful of candy. That was the last meeting together and the last time I saw Henry or any of the club members.

. . . .

CHAPTER 27

Grandmother's Medicine

About a month later, I found a new group of friends that were not involved in any type of criminal activity. We did more innocent things like jumping rope, hide-and-seek, playing house, and tossing rocks. Finally, I felt like a kid again. But that, too, did not last long because I got injured while playing a game of rock throwing with one of the kids in the neighborhood. On one particular day, we were playing "dodge the rock" game. The rule was, if you got hit with the rock, you were automatically out of the game. It was kind of like a game of dodgeball but with rocks. I stuck my head out from around a telephone pole, and the rock hit me in my face square between my eyes and smack-dab in the middle of my head, and I was knocked unconscious. All I remembered when I came to there was some stranger carrying me and a lot of kids following us to my house. When we got to my house, the stranger explained the situation to the best of his knowledge. My head was bleeding so bad blood was all over the man and dripping on the floor. My mom thanked the man and had him lay me on the couch while she ran to get a couple of bath towels. While she was running back down the stairs with the towels, she yelled to the man, "Could you do me a big favor?"

He replied, "Yes, how can I help?"

My mom said, "We do not have a phone, and I need someone to call me a cab." She gave him two nickels and told him to use them in the pay phone at the corner store. The man said he would be more than happy to make the call, but he refused the nickels. My mom said, "When you talk to them, please let them know it is an emergency, and our destination is Denver General Hospital." Then my mom said, "Please hurry, she is losing a lot of blood. I am having a problem stopping the bleeding."

The stranger hurried out the door, and my mom continued trying to get the bleeding to stop. The cab came rather quickly, and the cabdriver was extremely concerned about my well-being. He told my mom he hoped he did not get a ticket because he was definitely speeding to get me to the hospital. There was so much blood my mom had to apologize to the cabdriver because there was no way she could keep the blood from getting on his car seats. He was so nice he told my mom not to worry about the cab seats but to "take care of that little girl."

When we got to the hospital, my mother and I sat in the waiting room for about an hour. Then we were assigned to a room where we sat for almost five hours. My head had stopped bleeding, but the swelling in my head and face was so bad my mom said she could not recognize me anymore. She said she was afraid that the swelling had caused an infection because I had a fever. My mom tried repeatedly to talk to the nurse and asked to see the doctor, telling them, "My daughter is about to bleed to death." The nurse must have had a problem with my mother prior to that day because she had a real bad attitude and got real smart with my mother whenever she asked a question. She told my mom she was just going to have to wait her turn no matter how long it took, even though we had already waited five to six hours. My mom got frustrated, and she called my grandmother. She explained the problem she was having, trying to see a doctor.

My grandmother said, "Bring her to me right now." She told my mom to call her same cabdriver back and bring me to her house immediately. My mom called the cab and checked me out of the hospital. By that time, my eyes were swollen totally shut, and I had a big bag of infection on my face that was about the size of a big dill pickle. When we got to my grandmother's house, Gran said, "Her nose could possibly be broken, but since we cannot get a doctor to confirm that, I am going to have to use one of my home remedies and pray." Once we got settled in my grandmother's house, my grandmother yelled out to my grandfather, Curtis. That was my grandfather's first name (Curtis). She yelled, "You are going to have to go to the store and get this baby one of their biggest steaks they got!" She continued saying, "We have to put a steak on Lane's face. It is already full of infection, and we got to get the poison out."

Papa asked, "What kind of steak should I get?"

My grandmother replied, "Just make sure it is one of the top cuts of beef and one of the largest ones." Meanwhile, my grandmother was trying everything to stop the bleeding that had begun again. She eventually got the bleeding to stop again. By this time, I had two black eyes. When Papa made it back from the store with the steak, Gran put the meat right on top of the pickle-shaped bag of infection. It reached from the tip of my hairline to the end of my nose and reached from one side of my face to the other. Gran put some kind of ointment and oil on the wound after cleaning the area and tied the meat to my face with a roll of gauze. She wrapped the gauze around my head over and over again until she was sure the meat was securely in place. She said it was important to get it right because I had to keep the meat on my face for two weeks. I thought, *How in the world am I supposed to live like this?*

When I got enough nerve to go outside in the neighborhood, the kids would make jokes and laugh at me. I could not even get mad at them because I really did look crazy with a big piece of meat tied to my face. There were flies and gnats buzzing over my face all the time. It was so pitiful looking. I had to sleep and eat with that big, heavy meat on my face day and night. I tried to sneak a peek underneath the meat after about a week. What I saw scared me so bad I wanted to cry. It was so horrible! I prayed to God, "Please heal this thing on my face. Do not let me look like a monster, please." Much to my surprise, two weeks later when my grandmother removed the gauze and the steak from my face, there was no swelling or infection. Even my two black eyes were gone. My whole face had been healed. My grandmother's prayers and steak remedy worked. Our prayers had been answered. After that incident, I stopped playing in the neighborhood with the rock-slinging group of children.

· · · · · · · · · · · ·

CHAPTER 28

He Almost Hit Me

After getting hit in the face with the rock and having no success with my new group of friends, I gave up on trying to have friends and decided to just be alone. My mother was dating a new guy. His name was Richard Johnson Lewis, but we just called him RJ for short. He was a lightweight prize fighter; he was tall, handsome, and with a large, muscular body. He had light-brown, golden skin that looked beautiful. He had a great sense of humor; at least I thought he did. He was always making me laugh. I thought it would be nice if I could make him laugh and play a joke on him. One day when me, RJ, and my mom were all sitting around in the kitchen getting ready to eat dinner, RJ said he had to run upstairs and grab something. That's when I got the bright idea to play a trick on him. When he went to sit down in his chair, I walked behind him calmly and yanked the chair out from under him before he could sit down. He hit the floor hard, *bam*. I busted out laughing and jumping up and down, saying, "I got you. I pulled a joke on you." I thought he would get up and start laughing and saying, "Yes, you did. You got me." But instead, he got up with his fist balled up, ready to hit me. At that point, he brought his fist up in the air and was about to hit me with his fist.

My mom jumped and screamed, "No, stop! Do not hit her!" She jumped in front of me and blocked his fist from coming down on me. She yelled at him, "Stop!" And then she said, "Baby, she was just playing with you. She was not trying to hurt you. You play with her all the time. She is only a child trying to play with you and play jokes on you."

He was still furious with me and accused me of trying to break his back. He said, "I am a fighter for a living. I must stay in shape. You tried to break my back."

I was crying by that time. He scared me so bad. I knew if he would have hit me, I probably would have died. My mom told me to go up to my room. RJ never accepted my apology for playing the joke on him. After that incident, RJ never joked with me again. As a matter of fact, he did not really talk to me after that. He preferred that I stayed out of his sight. My mom made an announcement a couple months later that she was pregnant, and RJ was the daddy. He was in the room when Mom made the announcement with all my sisters around. He did not look too thrilled about the idea of becoming a father. I noticed that he stopped coming around as much. And the closer it got to the delivery date, the more I hardly saw him. Eventually, he left altogether. My mom went ahead and delivered a baby girl. This time, Mom brought the baby home. I finally had me a beautiful, brand-new baby sister. My mom named her Diane, and it looked like she loved Diane, but she was still praying for that baby boy. But now I was no longer the baby in the house; Diane was. We nicknamed Diane DD. I was in love with my new baby sister, DD. My mother taught me how to change her and feed her. I loved feeding and caring for her, as if she were my own child.

About a couple of months later, my mom said she was pregnant again. I had not seen a man at our house for a while. So I wondered who the daddy of this baby was. I wanted to ask her if RJ was the father, same as DD's. But she was going on and on about maybe this was going to be the boy that she had desperately wanted. I just forgot about asking her who the daddy was. It really did not matter to me. I was glad another baby was coming home. Fast-forwarding my life to about ten months later, my mom delivered another baby girl. Unfortunately, this baby did not make it home either. Much to Mom's disappointment, she had delivered another girl. Still not bearing a son, she was devastated, but I was eager to have another baby sister to care for. When my mom went to the hospital for delivery,

I was so excited for DD, and I thought it would be good for DD to have someone else to play with. When my mom returned from the hospital, she did not have the baby with her. I asked my mom, "Where is the baby?" She told me she had to leave the baby at the hospital because she already had too many children. I said, "That is what you said when you left the last one at the hospital." I did not understand what she was talking about. Why did she still want a boy if she had too many children? As I continued to question her, she said she was not in the mood to discuss the matter any further. All the confusion just made me love and protect DD even more, so I didn't ask any more questions or complain.

Three years had come and gone since we moved back in with our mom. I was enrolled in an elementary school about eight blocks from my house. I walked to school by myself every day because Rosie did not like me to be with her and her friends. I still did not have any good friends. Somehow, I had made it to the third grade. I only went to school for the morning classes, and I would leave in the afternoon. The only reason I went to school was to get some breakfast and lunch for me and DD. I would hang out in the neighborhood and would not come home until school was dismissed. That was how I kept my mom from knowing I was not in school. At breakfast or lunchtime, I would wrap DD's food in a paper napkin and take it home to her. I always made sure she had food every time I had food. DD had turned about three years old, and she was getting into everything. Her hair had grown so long. She had beautiful, long black hair, like my mother. Sometimes she would let me brush and comb her hair and put it in a ponytail. Months turned into years, and DD was steadily growing. I enjoyed playing, teaching, and caring for DD. I felt like her mom. One day, DD was standing at the top of the stairs, attempting to go down the stairs. When she missed the first step, she would have hit her head on the concrete steps. When I saw her falling, I did some quick thinking and jumped and grabbed her before her head could hit the steps, but my head hit the steps and wall. I knew I could take a fall. Plus, I felt like it was my job to protect her from any harm.

Meanwhile, my mom was getting depressed. She was still disappointed because she did not have a baby boy. She got depressed and did not sing or whistle anymore. She stayed in her bedroom most of the time. I tried talking to her by asking her how she was doing or if I could get her something. She would not answer me; instead, she would just stare into space. She was behaving like she did years ago when she had a broken jaw from the bad beating when I was five years old.

CHAPTER 29

. . . .

I Dare You

After a couple of months of the silent treatment from my mom, I decided to try to make her laugh or make her pay me some attention. I knew what I was going to say sounded stupid, but I just wanted to get some type of reaction from her. There was an iron sitting on the ironing board in the front room where we were sitting. I walked right up to her and got in her face and said, "Mom, I dare you to pick that iron up and throw it through the picture window." The window was about the size of a large chalkboard. Mama was sitting on the couch with her back to the window.

She opened her mouth and said, "Lane, do not ever dare anyone to do anything."

I was shocked she was talking to me. She was responding to what I said. I thought, *Well, at least she is talking to me now.* So I kept the conversation going.

Then she said, "Where do you want me to throw it?"

I thought, *Well, she is still talking,* so I said something that I thought would be too crazy to ever think about doing, and then we could continue to communicate after I said those crazy words. I said, "I dare you to throw it through the front picture window." The window was right in back of the couch. She was sitting on it at the time I dared her. My mom got up and walked over to the corner of the room where the iron and ironing board were located. She picked up the iron. I was hoping any minute that she would start laughing or saying something like "I tricked you" or anything humorous. Even if she questioned my motives for requesting such a dumb thing, I just wanted to get a breakthrough and have a conversation with my mom. That was all. Instead, my mom walked to the center of the room with the iron in her hand. She just stood there looking at the window for about a minute. At that point, I realized my mom was doing something I told her to do. It was like she gave me some power. I could not stop myself from egging her on, saying, "Mama, I double dare you." I barely got the last word out of my mouth when I saw the iron flying through the air toward the big window. It was a loud, horrifying sound as the iron busted through the glass. In a snap, I saw the glass crack and shatter. It was like looking at something in slow motion. There were big chunks of glass inside and outside the house. I yelled, "Oh my god, Mom! You did it. You really threw the iron through the window." I was standing there with my eyes bucked and my hands over my mouth in shock. It was wintertime. Snow was on the ground, and it was snowing on that day. It snowed all the time in Denver, and the wind started blowing the snow in the house.

Then my mom turned to me and said in a calm voice, "Laney, never dare anyone to do anything." She went on to say, "I hope this has taught you a lesson."

I said to myself, "Well, yes, I learned a lesson all right. And that lesson was, my mom is crazy."

Our neighbors came running to the front of the house, wondering what had happened with that loud crashing sound. My mom looked out the window and saw all the neighbors gathering around and standing in front of our yard. She yelled out, "What are you looking at? Haven't you ever seen a broken window before?" The people became fearful because Mom yelled at them. She said, "All yah need to get off my lawn and get away from my house." It was snowing outside, and the snow blew right inside the front room, onto the couch, and on the floor. The window stayed like that all day and night until the next day when the project maintenance man came and boarded it up.

After the broken window incident, my mom started isolating herself even more. She started staying in her room and not coming out other than to eat or to go to the bathroom. I was still attending the nearby elementary school, playing hooky and bringing my lunch home for DD. I would do my best for a third grader to make sure DD was not hungry. Although I still ate out of the trash cans sometimes, I just could not see letting my baby sister, DD, eating food from the trash, and I did everything I could to make sure she did not. I wondered whatever happened to my other two baby sisters that did not come home. So I prayed that they would get a good mommy and a daddy that would make them lunch and breakfast every day.

CHAPTER 30

. . . .

They're Taking DD Away

After the incident with my mom and the broken window, it was only a matter of a few months before the social workers and the medical team had returned to take my mom back to the hospital for more evaluations. Mama did not put up a fuss or fight this time. I think she was tired of trying to make things work on her own. Unfortunately, Mom going back into the hospital meant my sisters and I were all going back into the foster care system again, and this time, that included DD. This would be DD's first time in a foster home. I asked the social worker to put DD in the same foster home with me and Rosie. I had become so attached to DD, just like I was with Rosie, but my social worker said no. DD had to be placed in a separate home because DD was much younger than me and Rosie. That meant DD was going into a different foster home all by herself. The social worker told me that she had worked hard to keep me and Rosie together, and I needed to be thankful for what I had. I was very thankful that Rosie and I got to stay together, but I was so sad that they took DD away from me. I worried if she was eating good or getting a whipping for peeing in the bed. I worried that she might get bullied and no one would be there to help her. I had all those thoughts going through my head concerning DD. I felt so helpless.

We gathered all our belongings and started preparing for our move. There were several ladies each in different cars. A tall white lady said, "Girls, you all have been assigned to different case workers.

When I call your name, raise your hand. Your case worker or social worker will introduce herself and help you load your things into her car." When Rosie's and my name were called, we raised our hands. The tall white lady that was speaking said she was Rosie's and my social worker. She introduced herself as Mrs. Clark. She helped me and Rosie load our things into her car. My baby sister, DD, was put in another car, and all three of my other sisters—Lena, Raney, and Ommie—got into a car together. I heard their social worker say they were going to an all-girls group home. The medical team put my mom and her things in the van. We all said our goodbyes and hugged. I was so sad for DD. She was the only one in a car by herself. She was not crying. She just had a look on her face of being confused.

As we were driving away, I could not help but have some flashbacks of the good and bad times spent in the project. I had never felt like this before. Maybe it was because my social worker said we were going to a permanent foster home. That sounded so final. I looked at Rosie and repeated what the social worker said. I asked Rosie, "Did you hear what the social worker said? That this is going to be permanent?" I was trying to make light of the fact that we were moving again and Mom was going back into the hospital.

Rosie was not interested in me making light of the situation or putting a positive spin on the conversation. Instead, she said, "Here we go again." Rosie was not smiling. She had an angry look on her face. Rosie was always a serious child. I always felt like it was my job to make her laugh or get her in a good mood. I think I could have been one of the youngest comedians because Rosie was a tough crowd to make laugh. And I got a lot of practice with Rosie because she worked so hard to keep me safe. I thought the least thing that I could do was to make her smile.

CHAPTER 31

. . . .

Permanent Foster Home

As Rosie and I arrived in the neighborhood of our permanent foster home, we observed the homes and lawns. All the homes were brick and well-kept. The lawns were manicured, and there were nice cars parked in front of the houses. Our social worker, Mrs. Clark, said we would probably like this home because this home had a lot to offer us as children. I did not know what she meant by "a lot to offer," but it sounded good. When we reached our new home, Mrs. Clark was in the process of bringing the car to a complete stop when she spoke in a loud voice, "Oh, look, there is Mrs. Graves now. She is standing right there on the front porch." She said, "She must have been waiting on you girls." I looked to see her, and I saw a white lady standing on the porch. It was a two-story reddish-brown brick house with awnings over the windows. Down the porch steps came the white lady rushing up to our car. As she continued to approach the car, Mrs. Clark said in a soft whisper, "That is your new foster mom, Mrs. Graves."

As soon as Mrs. Graves reached us, she had her arms wide open and stretched out. She grabbed Rosie first and gave her a big hug, then she hugged me and asked, "Who is Rosie, and who's Elaine?" We replied, saying our names. She said, "Girls, welcome to your new home." She gave us both another hug, seeming so excited to see us. As we were standing in the front yard getting acquainted with each other, Rosie and I were both looking to see if there were any children in the neighborhood. Mrs. Graves suddenly said, "Oh, I almost forgot. You need to come inside so you can meet my husband, Mr. Graves." Mrs. Graves was a pretty lady. She had a medium build and straight black hair that came to her shoulders. She had lipstick and makeup on, a beautiful dress, and some pump shoes. She was looking as though she was going to church. Mrs. Graves seemed extremely excited to see us and happy to get foster children.

As we began to walk up a few stairs onto the front porch, I could hear dogs barking in the background. I asked, "Do you have dogs, Mrs. Graves?"

She replied, "Yes, dear, I have two. And right after you meet Mr. Graves, I will take you to meet my two best friends, named Roy and Susie." She said those were the dogs' names.

As we entered the sitting room, I saw a staircase to my right leading upstairs, and to my left was a big room called the living room. My eyes were drawn straight to a painting that hung over the fireplace in the living room. It was a painting of a white boy. He was dressed in blue with his foot of on a rock. It was a picture of a boy from back in the colonial days. It was a large painting, about twenty-four by thirty-six inches or larger. I did not know what intrigued me about that painting, which captured my undivided attention, but for some reason, all the other voices in the room disappeared as I stared at that painting. And then Mrs. Graves called out in a loud voice, "Roy!" That was Mr. Graves's first name. She said, "The girls are here." Mrs. Graves yelled out again, "Come on down and meet Elaine and Rosie."

I heard a deep, commanding voice say, "Okay, I am on my way. Just one moment, please." Then I saw this tall, well-dressed, handsome man walking down the staircase and entering the sitting room. He had a big smile with a thin mustache over the top of his lip. His eyes were bright, and he had nice, clear skin. He had a medium-brown complexion and looked to be about six feet tall. He had some sort of hat on. The hat looked like something I had seen in a parade before. The color was red, and it was shaped like a small upside-down bucket with a tassel hanging down the side of it. He also had a jacket on that had some type of emblems on it. Mr. Graves introduced himself with a big smile and asked, "Which one is Rosie, and which one is Elaine?" We introduced ourselves and continued to observe our new family. Mr. Graves said he knew we probably had a lot of questions, but he had to leave. He said he had a meeting that he must attend. He said, "That is why I am dressed this way, wearing my Shriners hat and my Shriners jacket. I am a member of the Shriners." He went on to say, "As a matter of fact, I am the guest speaker for the meeting today. So please understand that I have to run for now, and unfortunately, I have to go to work tomorrow at Stapleton Airport." He said he painted airplanes and signs for a living. He continued to say if we did not mind waiting until the weekend; he would be off work. This way, he said he would be free from distractions and would give us an opportunity to sit down and get to know each other. After our short meet-and-greet with Mr. Graves, he said he would be on his way and Mrs. Graves could take it from here. Mr. Graves gave Mrs. Graves a kiss on the lips. He then turned his attention to Mrs. Clark, our social worker. He thanked her for her hard work and shook her hand. Then he was off to his Shriners meeting.

Mrs. Clark said, "Well, it looks like my job is done here. So I guess I will be on my way. I wish you girls the best with your new family." Then she leaned over to me and Rosie and gave us a hug. She looked us in the eye and said, "You know, I am only a phone call away if you ever need me. But I think you girls have found the home you always wanted." Then the social worker said her goodbyes and left.

Mrs. Graves seemed to be a caring, loving woman. She asked Rosie and I if we were hungry and if she could get us something to drink. My eyes lit up, and a big smile came across my face. Rosie even smiled a little. Rosie and I answered yes! We would like something to eat and drink. She said, "Okay, let us take your things upstairs to your room and then get something to eat. We will unpack those things later, and then you all can take your baths and put on the new pajamas that I bought you." As we followed Mrs. Graves up the stairs, she said, "First, let me show you around upstairs. Our room is on the left." We preceded into their room, which was large with a picture window with a view of Vine Street. They had a nice, big bed with matching spread curtains. We got a good look, and she escorted us out of their bedroom and back into the hall. There was the guest room in the center of the hall. Mrs. Graves was proud to show us how hard she worked decorating and matching the light fixtures in the room. As we left the guest room, our bedroom was straight ahead. The bathroom was on the right. We peeked in the bathroom as Mrs. Graves was pointing out where to put our toothbrushes and the location of our towel racks we were assigned. The bathroom walls were an off-white color, and the sink and bathtub were an olive green. There were small, soft rugs on the floor with one small window at the rear of the bathroom above the toilet. Inside the bathroom was a small closet. Mrs. Graves called it a linen closet. I had never seen so many washcloths and towels in my life unless it was in a store. They were stacked neatly one on top of the other in a row.

Finally, we entered our bedroom. The first thing I saw were two bunk beds. I started having flashbacks of my past. I remembered the foster parents that made me eat my cornflakes in water. Although I knew Mr. and Mrs. Graves were not the same bad foster parents, I still felt like something bad was going to happen. I began to get nervous and started breathing. I felt like I could not move. I just stood there staring at the bed. Mrs. Graves and Rosie were leaving the room when Mrs. Graves noticed me staring at the bed. She said, "Elaine, are you going to just stand there, gawking at the bed? Or are you going to go downstairs with us to get something to eat?"

The mention of food was all it took to get my attention. I quickly snapped out of my deep stare. I yelled, "Yes! I am coming with you." As I was leaving the room, I took one more look, noticing the beautiful mirror, table, and chair set that was next to the window. It was made of brown wood with a big, round mirror connected to the table with two drawers, one on each side. The chair was like a soft bench. It looked like a place where movie stars would put on their makeup. Then I took one quick glimpse out the window. There were two brown dogs. They were barking and running around a big tree in the fenced yard.

I quickly joined Rosie and Mrs. Graves as we made our way through the hall and halfway down the staircase covered with carpet. I noticed a small, round stained-glass window at eye level right before the staircase curved. From there, we followed her into the sitting room. Mrs. Graves yelled out, "Okay, girls, now is time for me to take you on a quick tour to the rest of the house." She walked us straight into the front room that was opposite the sitting room. On my left was a big picture window with some nice curtains draped over the window. Then there was that painting of the boy in blue that I liked. It was hanging over the fireplace. And to my right, in the front room, was a beautiful living room set—a couch and two chairs and a coffee table. Straight ahead opposite the window was the dining room. There was a fully stocked bar to the right. In the center of the dining room was a large chandelier hanging from the ceiling. Right below the chandelier was a beautiful dining-room table with all the table settings. There was also a door to exit from the dining room right into the kitchen, but for some reason, Mrs. Graves took us back the way we came.

We passed one more door on our way to the kitchen. I inquired Mrs. Graves, "Where does this door lead to?"

She said, "Oh, that's the basement door. I do not have time to show you girls the basement right now. We will get to that later, but for now, let us get something to eat." We continued into the kitchen. It was a nice kitchen with yellow curtains hanging at the windows. They had a big stove next to the sink and a refrigerator on the same side where the kitchen table was located, to my left next to a large cabinet. When she opened the cabinet, it was full of food, like the grocery store. The kitchen was not that big, but you could tell they had a lot of money. She asked what we would like to have, hamburgers, hot dogs, or something else. "Wow," I said to myself, "so many choices." I loved hot dogs, so I chose hot dogs. She cooked the hot dogs in an electric hot-dog grill. As if that was not enough, Mrs. Graves also started cooking burgers and french fries to make sure we would get full. That was when I knew we had hit the jackpot of all foster homes. She was cutting up the potatoes because we said french fries. Mrs. Graves literally started peeling potatoes and cutting them into strips and began cooking them right there. While the hot dogs were in the grilling container, the burgers were in the skillet. She put the buns in a skillet and browned them. I continued to look in amazement as she sliced tomatoes and chopped onions and sliced pickles. She arranged each in its own bowl. Then she placed the bowls on a round tray that moved. She called the tray a lazy Susie. When everything was ready, Mrs. Graves said now we could help ourselves.

She had set the table with ketchup, mustard, and mayonnaise, asking us if we would like pop, milk, water, iced tea, or juice. Rosie chose pop; I chose iced tea because I never had iced tea before. Once we got our plates filled with the hot dogs, hamburgers, and fries, Rosie and I were just looking at each other, as if to say, "Are we dreaming? Is this real?" I had never seen anyone do all that for hot dogs and french fries. She told us to have a seat, that she was going to say a prayer over the food. We all sat at the table where Mrs. Graves had put napkins on each person's plate. Rosie and I removed the napkins and set them on the side of our plates. Mrs. Graves instructed us to put the napkins on our laps and to keep our elbows off the table and to please not talk with our mouths full. I thought, *I know she is white, but none of the other foster moms made us do this.* Not even the white ones had these kinds of rules or manners. Rosie and I had no problem following the instructions, though it was going to take a little time to get used to.

After we finished eating and doing the dishes, Mrs. Graves said it's time for us to go outside in the back yard to meet the dogs, Roy and Susie. As we exited the kitchen, we entered the back porch. To my left was a long, square white freezer. There were a lot of other things like rakes, dog food, and all sorts of tools on shelves and on the floor. As soon as Mrs. Graves opened the door to the back porch, two beautiful brown dogs ran up to her. She was calling out their names. "Roy and Susie, calm down," she repeated. She said to the dogs, "I want you to meet two new members of our family, Rosie and Elaine." These dogs looked different from the dogs in the projects I was used to seeing. I asked Mrs. Graves what type of dogs they were. She responded, "They're cocker spaniels. Roy is a boy dog, and Susie is the female."

I asked her, "Do they bite?"

She responded, "No, they do not bite. They just like to play."

I thought, *That is good. I will be more than happy to play with them.*

As we walked through the backyard, I noticed the garage was built out of brick and an incinerator at the back of the yard next to the fence. The incinerator was used to burn trash. And there was a big tree that sat smack-dab in the middle of the yard. The branches on the tree were so big. They drooped and leaned on to the back-porch roof. The branches extended all the way up to our bedroom window. That meant someone could climb the tree onto the roof. There was an alley right outside the gate. was. Our house was only a couple of houses from the corner of Thirty-Second in Vine Street.

Now with our tour being finished, we had completed our lunch. Mrs. Graves told us we could go outside and sit on the front porch. There we could sit and familiarize ourselves with our surroundings. She said she was going to go and start preparing dinner. I said to myself, "Now I know this is a dream. She is going to prepare dinner. We just ate lunch." Rosie and I went ahead and sat on the front porch. There were a couple of chairs and a table on the porch. As we sat and observed the neighborhood, which again was well-kept, we started seeing quite a few children outside their homes playing. We could see a sign at the corner saying One Way. There was another sign saying Thirty-Second and Vine. We could not help but notice all the traffic on Thirty-Second Avenue. Rosie and I stayed on the porch observing, talking, and laughing for a couple hours until Mrs. Graves told us that we could go ahead and take our baths early since it was our first day but not to put our pajamas on until we were ready for bed.

By the time we got finished with our baths, Mrs. Graves was calling us for dinner. She said Mr. Graves would not be joining us for dinner because he had to work late. Rosie and I joined Mrs. Graves for dinner. We noticed again there were lots of forks, spoons, and knives. There was more silverware than we had at lunchtime. Plus, there were two empty glasses both filled with ice. I inquired, "Why do we have two glasses, Mrs. Graves?"

She said, "One glass is your water glass. The other is for the beverage of your choice. Are there any other questions about the table setting?"

Rosie said, "Yes. Why do we have so many forks and spoons?"

She replied, "This is a semiformal dinner setting. Every utensil on this table has a purpose." She explained how you start with the fork in the center that was a salad fork, working your way to the outside to the dinner fork. "On the other side of the plate are your spoons. The first is for your tea, then soup or whatever you need to stir. Then you have a butter knife and a steak knife."

I said, "Wow, that is a lot to remember."

She said, "You just as well get used to remembering all of the place setting that includes the silverwares setting because we eat this way every day. And when Roy eats with us, you need to be on your best manners."

I said to myself, "Oh, my goodness, why?" But then she served us a meal that was fit for a king—baked potatoes, asparagus, steak, salad, and apple pie à la mode, at least that was what she called it.

After a wonderful dinner, we helped wash the pots and pans and put the dishes in the dishwasher. I had never seen a dishwasher let alone used one. When the kitchen was clean, Mrs. Graves said we could sit and talk in the front room. We instead retired to our bedroom to continue our conversation. Rosie and I both needed time alone to talk to each other and process our new foster family. We stayed up half the night talking until we fell asleep.

. . . .

CHAPTER 32

Second Day with the Graves

Rosie and I woke up to a knock on the door, saying, "Girls, breakfast is ready. You need to get up and get dressed and come down and join us for breakfast." We hurried up and got dressed. Once we were seated at the kitchen table, Mrs. Graves began putting our breakfast on the table. Again, I was shocked at how much food she had prepared. There was bacon, sausages, pancakes, toast, hash brown potatoes, scrambled eggs, poached eggs, and sunny-side-up eggs. Mr. Graves's favorite eggs were poached eggs. He joined us for breakfast this morning. He had his poached eggs along with sliced fruit, toast, and juice. He did not eat much for a tall man. When he finished eating, he started reading the newspaper.

The breakfast table was set just like I had seen in a magazine for rich people. The napkins were placed on the table along with the silverware. By now Rosie and I had started getting the hang of it. We had placed our napkins on our laps, remembered, to sit up straight, selected and used our utensils in the proper manner, and made sure we did not talk with our mouths full. We did surprisingly good on our first breakfast with Mr. Graves. Mr. Graves did not have any complaints about us. He asked us and Mrs. Graves what she had planned for us that afternoon. She responded, "I plan to take the girls shopping. They need a whole new wardrobe."

Mr. Graves said, "Make sure you have the checkbook and get them whatever they need."

Mrs. Graves did not drive, so we had to catch the city bus. I had never ridden on a city bus, but I was looking forward to it. Once we were aboard the bus, it headed toward downtown Denver. I noticed that all the people on the bus were white except for me and Rosie, and they were looking at me and Rosie very strangely. And after a while, a couple of white ladies came up and said to Mrs. Graves, "They are very well-mannered" and "Here is a little something to help you out." They were giving Mrs. Graves money, as if she needed it. Mrs. Graves never said a word. She just smiled and said, "Thank you." I did not understand why they were giving her money. I started thinking they did that to all the mothers whose children were well-behaved on the bus.

We got off the bus in downtown Denver in front of several large department stores. Once we were in the beautiful stores, Mrs. Graves said, "I know there is a lot to see, but we are here for one thing, and that is to get you girls a decent wardrobe. So you are going to have to try on some clothes and shoes to make sure they fit and that you like them." We must have gone to seven different stores. We were shopping up a storm, trying on clothes and shoes and purchasing whatever we needed. We all had our arms full of big bags. We shopped to the point Mrs. Graves said, "Okay, enough shopping for today. Let us go get something to eat." She took us to a restaurant downtown next to one of the department stores. I cannot remember the restaurant; I just know that was when I fell in love with waiters and waitresses. I had never been to a restaurant where people waited on you and treated you so nicely. After resting and finishing up our lunch, we gathered our things and got back on the bus headed for home.

I could hardly wait to go inside the house and try on all my wonderful clothing. As Rosie and I were trying on our clothing, Mrs. Graves yelled up the stairs and spoke, "I want you girls to come down and show me how your clothes fit and look." So Rosie and I tried on each garment and modeled in front of Mrs. Graves to get her approval. She agreed with our taste in clothing and gave her stamp of approval. She said once we got a little older, we could go shopping without her since we did so well.

CHAPTER 33

. . . .

School Enrollment

Now we had been residing with the Graves for about a month when Mrs. Graves announced that the time had come for me and Rosie to get registered for school. The name of our new school was Columbine Elementary located in East Central Denver. This school was about a mile from our house. There were no school buses or any form of transportation for students at that time. So that meant we were going to be required to walk every day no matter if there was rain, sleet, or snow; there was no such thing as a snow day. Mrs. Graves said she had all our shot records and necessary paperwork to get us enrolled in school. But this school required an appointment with a school counselor prior to enrollment. Mrs. Graves had no problem supporting us in every way she could concerning school.

Once we arrived at the school, I could see this was a much larger school than what I was used to attending. It was about four stories tall and red brick with lots of windows. As we entered the hallways, there were only a few parents with their children on that day. We were being directed by a teacher to go straight to the room where the counselor resided. We entered the meeting room and had a seat in front of a desk. There was a middle-aged white lady sitting at the desk. She welcomed us into the room and introduced herself. She said her name was Mrs. Smith, and she was my counselor. She seemed to be in a hurry because she was speaking so fast. Then she said, "I am sorry, but I am running short on time today. So I am going to just get to the point." Then she asked me what I wanted to be when I grow up. I told her I wanted to be a housewife, like Mrs. Graves. Her response was, "Yes, I understand every little girl wants to have children and get married. But what are your hopes and dreams in life as a professional worker?"

I did not have a clue what she was talking about and answered with, "I just want to have a husband and be the best mother I can be. That's it." I felt like she was trying to convince me that I should want more out of life, but all I ever wanted was to have a family. Everything else would work itself out. I began to get agitated with the counselor, Mrs. Smith. She acted like my hopes and dreams were not good enough for her. She finally gave up trying to convince me that I should want more out of life, and she went ahead and assigned me to a teacher. I did not think Mrs. Smith knew much about her job by the way she questioned me about my future. But come to find out, she had figured me out surprisingly well because the classroom and the teacher she assigned me to was perfect for me. My teacher's name was Mrs. Carter. She was very patient with me and understood my awkward way of learning. After a while, I began to understand English, math, and social studies. Before Mrs. Carter, I did not think I could learn these tough subjects, but Mrs. Carter had a way of teaching me that made it fun to learn. By the third semester, I was bringing home As, Bs, and Cs. Before Mrs. Carter, I was glad if I got a C or a D in class. Duddy, my neighborhood friend, was partially responsible in helping me get those good grades also. Duddy was my own personal tutor. Rosie was also doing well in school.

I found myself doing even better after meeting my neighbor Justin. Justin was trying out for the World Olympics and had all types of training equipment at his home. Justin was training to compete as a gymnast. He taught me how to jump on his trampoline, balance bars, and swing on the hanging bars. The most important thing Justin taught me was how to meditate. He taught me to meditate at night before I went to bed concerning whatever I wanted to accomplish. He said if I thought about it hard enough before I fell asleep that the answer would come to me in my sleep or the next day. After some practice jumping on the trampoline, I took Justin's advice and began meditating right before I fell asleep. Then one night, I had a dream that I was jumping on the trampoline, doing backflips and triple summersaults, and landing on my feet like a professional. The next day, I ran to Justin's house ready to try out what I had dreamed. To my shock, I was actually doing better than I thought. I was imitating all of Justin's moves, including the triple summersault. I mastered the meditation sleeping technique to the point I started using it for taking tests at school. I would meditate on an assignment, and then when I took the test, the answers would come to me. I got so good at it that I did not worry about learning anything. All I had to do was dream about it no matter what it was.

CHAPTER 34

. . . .

Martin Luther King Unity March

Rosie and I continued to flourish all through the school year while residing with Mr. and Mrs. Graves. As we neared the end of the school year, my teacher, Mrs. Carter, made an announcement. She said that there was a man named Martin Luther King having a unity march. She said he was asking different cities to come together and march for a show of unity. I remembered that name from where my grandmother showed me the riots on TV in Alabama, so I intuitively knew Mr. King was someone immensely powerful. But I was confused as why my white history teacher was so interested in this march. I had not seen any discrimination at my school or in my city. I asked Mrs. Carter why they were having a march in Denver. She explained to me and my fellow students, saying, "Although we may not have segregation here in Denver, Colorado, that does not mean our brothers and sisters in other cities and states are not being denied their rights." For example, she said many people of color in the Southern states were still being oppressed. She went on to say, "They are not in an integrated setting as we are, and because I am a history teacher, I feel it is a great opportunity to experience and be a part of making history." And then Mrs. Carter said, "Remember, you always want to be on the right side of history."

I asked Mrs. Carter, "Is there going to be a lot of people in the march?"

She replied, "We are hoping for thousands to turn out." Then she said, "Now who wants to participate in the freedom march?" I raised my hand straight up high, then I looked around the room, and all the students in the room had their hands raised also. I was shocked because I was the only Black student in the class, but all the white kids had their hands raised too. Mrs. Carter got so excited. She said, "Well, I guess we are all going to go to the march." She went on to explain the information on how we would assemble the day of the march and how she would continue to give us updates until the actual day. She continued to explain how we would be leaving from our school and joining in with other people as we walked down the streets for miles until we reached the capitol building in downtown Denver.

When she said how far we were going to be walking, my imagination started going crazy, remembering pictures of what I saw on TV in Alabama with dogs barking and police with clubs in hand trying to hurt the marchers. Thinking about all that made me inquire further. I asked Mrs. Carter, "Will the police have dogs and try to stop us like they did in the South?"

She replied, "No, Elaine, this is a unity freedom march. And we are in Denver, Colorado, not Alabama. Rest assured, you will be safe."

I replied, "Okay."

Mrs. Carter said, "Different cities all over the United States will be coming together in a show of unity across America. The main march will be held in Alabama, where Dr. Martin Luther King will be speaking. All of the marchers are marching on the same day at the same time in each city to show solidarity for freedom and equality. You do not have to worry about the police and dogs in Denver because we are already a free state. That is why we can go anywhere anytime we want. No matter what your race or religion is, we have equal rights in Denver. That is why we are marching for our sisters and brothers to have those same rights that we take for granted every day."

I said Mrs. Carter was a good teacher, but now I knew she was a good human being also. Then Mrs. Carter said, "Another thing, you do not have to worry about losing class time. Everyone who goes to the march will get class credit for their participation. I am asking each student to write a short story about their experience concerning the march, and you will get extra class credit for it. The one who has the best story will get a chance to read their story out loud in class and receive one of my blue ribbons." Just like I said, Mrs. Carter always made learning fun and meaningful.

It was about a week later when the anticipated day had arrived. We were in our classroom on the third floor, where we could see all the people outside our window. They had gathered on the streets below in the front of our school. Mrs. Carter had been working hard with the other teachers. They were putting cold drinks and snacks on a wagon. They wanted to make sure we all stayed hydrated as we marched. After everything was prepared, we were ready to go. We were told to go downstairs and stay close together while we held one another's hands. Mrs. Carter said if we felt like it, we could join in singing the freedom songs at any time. Finally, we were given the green light to start marching. We were instructed to walk in the middle of the street. The police had blocked the intersections to make sure the traffic was halted. As we continued marching through the streets, we started off in what I thought was a large group, but it was small compared to how it grew after we had walked about a mile. By the time we were only halfway there, there were so many people behind us. We could not see the end of the march.

As we were approaching downtown, there were people flowing in from different sides of the streets onto the main street that led to the capitol. We made our way through the crowd until we got in front of the capitol. There were so many people we had to go toward the back of the crowd. That meant it was hard for me to see and hear who was giving their speeches, on the capitol steps. I was so short compared to the adults in the crowd. It made it difficult for me to see over their shoulders, but I was just as grateful for the experience and hearing the voices of the speakers and standing in the midst of thousands of people for the cause of making America a better place to live. It was an awesome experience, and I can honestly say, I had part in making history that day.

When it was all over, we returned to our school safe and sound. It was reported that on that day, there were no acts of violence at the march. Just peace and unity was reported by the news. I wrote about my experience at the Martin Luther King march and got an A plus for my story, but unfortunately, I got a D on my grammar and punctuation. Another student won the blue ribbon and read his story aloud in front of the class. I shared my experience with my best friend Duddy. After sharing my story with her, she thought I was so brave to take part in the march. As a matter of fact, Duddy let me know that she had begun to admire my strengths that I never knew I had and continually reminded me how it took a strong person to have gone through what I went through in my childhood and not be bitter and angry. I was really thankful for my friendship with Duddy as I was constantly struggling to make good choices.

CHAPTER 35

. . . .

Life-Changing Experiences

Finally, school is out, and Mr. and Mrs. Graves had decided to reward me and Rosie by taking us on a trip with them to Albuquerque, New Mexico. Mr. Graves said we would be staying with one of his family members for a week. He also mentioned that we would be driving in his gray station wagon. I was excited about going on my first trip out of Colorado. I knew I was going to miss my friend Duddy; I wished we could take her with us. At first, I thought we were going to leave the United States and go to the country of Mexico. Mrs. Graves explained that Albuquerque, New Mexico, was part of the United States. I thought I was just part of making history with the Martin Luther King march. Now I was going to experience another culture while on vacation. As we were getting prepared for the trip as the day approached, Mrs. Graves took me and Rosie shopping for new clothing, essential products, and luggage. Money was no problem for Mr. and Mrs. Graves. Rosie and I could barely sleep in anticipation of the trip.

On the morning of the trip, I went into the kitchen and saw Mrs. Graves leaning over a big picnic basket. She was busy making sandwiches and filling the basket full of food and drinks. She had everything in that basket, everything from chips, dip, fried chicken, salad, fruit, and every kind of drink you could think of. As evening fell, Mrs. Graves told us to hurry up and put the finishing touches on our packing. She instructed us to put our luggage at the front door.

She went on to say Mr. Graves was very particular and likes every-thing in order especially when he was loading up the car for a trip. She said, "You girls will be asleep when Roy starts the loading. That is why your luggage needs to be at the door. You know how Roy is. He believes in that old saying that the early bird gets the worm." About 10:00 p.m., Mrs. Graves instructed me and Rosie to go to bed. She wanted to make sure we were rested for the trip. Rosie and I went to bed, but I did not know how much sleep we got because we stayed up talking half the night away until we fell asleep.

Before we knew it, Mrs. Graves was saying, "Girls, it is time to get up." We got right up although we were very tired. We grabbed our small bags and hurried down the stairs and got in the car. We each had a bag full of games, puzzles, cards, paper, pencils, and defi-nitely my crayons. As soon as Rosie and I got in the car, we fell asleep. We were awakened to Mrs. Graves's voice as Mr. Graves pulled the car into a rest stop. Mrs. Graves said, "Girls, this is a nice, clean rest stop. So get your toothbrushes and change of clothes. You can freshen up, and then we'll get back on the road." Once we were back in the car and on our way, Mrs. Graves asked, "Is anybody hungry?" She started naming off different foods she brought for breakfast, like cereal, milk, orange juice, and bacon and boiled eggs. The cooler that was filled with all the cold drinks was sitting on the floor between me and Rosie. We were passing food and drinks back and forth until everyone got what they wanted. When we finished eating, my eyes were glued out the window for a good while, but there was not a lot to see on the open highway, just a lot of dirt and flat land. Rosie and I took this opportunity to play some of our games, and before we knew it, we were having a wonderful time in the back seat playing all types of games, like who could name the most cars that looked alike. Then I would draw pictures and color, while Rosie wrote in her diary. Then we would switch up and play another game of old maid using the cards. We rode for hours and hours that seemed like days and days.

We drove until we reached an area that looked like we were in the desert. That was the town Mr. Graves decided to stop and get gas. The gas pump was literally at an old, scrubby-looking white man's house. He had a gas pump like I had never seen before. It looked like a big upside-down water bottle sitting on a stand. The bottle was made of glass and full to the top with gasoline. When the gas was being pumped, I could see the big bubbles come up through the glass container. As we got deeper into the desert, it was beautiful. There were all kinds of cactus. Some were different colors and different shapes. As we entered the city limits of Albuquerque, there was a lady and some children outside of an adobe house. The lady was sitting on the ground, making some type of food over a fire. I asked Mr. Graves if we would be staying in an adobe house with his relatives. He replied no. He said, "There are only a few people who still live in adobe houses and cook outside."

I said, "I sure would like to get close enough to see someone cook outside."

He replied, "Do not worry, you will get a chance when we get to my family's house. There are a couple of Mexican settlers still living and cooking in adobe houses in the area where we will be staying."

When we arrived, Mr. Graves's family was very hospitable. They welcomed us with open arms and showed us to our room. The only problem was, they had no children, and there were no children in the neighborhood to play with. So Rosie and I had nothing to do during our entire stay there but the same thing we did in the car on our way there—which was to play our board games and old maid card game—sing songs, and go outside and stand around in the heat. Standing outside in the heat was not the best option, so playing indoors was our world for just about the whole time we were there. As it got closer to the time to go home, Rosie and I complained to Mrs. Graves how we had not had a chance to do or see anything the entire time we were there. Mrs. Graves said she would talk to Mr. Graves, and maybe on our way out, they could show us the downtown area, and we could see some of the people in the adobe houses. At the end of our stay, Mr. Graves and Mrs. Graves kept their word and took us to downtown Albuquerque. Although there was not a lot to see, they let us get out the car and go inside a small restaurant. We all got ice cream cones. Then they drove to one of the adobe houses. There, a lady was sitting outside on the ground with her legs crossed. She was crushing corn in a bowl and making corn tortilla patties. I wanted to ask the lady some questions, but she did not speak English. It was an experience I would never forget. Standing there looking at the lady cook reminded me of what I saw at the Denver Museum of Natural History. I could not believe that people still lived like that.

After being very thankful for all I saw and experienced, it was time to go. We all got back in the car and headed back home to Denver. On the way back, I saw something else I would never forget, a sunset that was so beautiful it was hard to describe. There were cactus in all colors scattered across the landscape. There were yellow, green, red, and purple. In the forefront of the sunset stood a beautiful cactus. In the distance was an orange, golden, crimson sunset with the brown earth beneath it all. That picture stuck in my mind. I began gathering my pencils, paper, and crayons to try and capture what I had just seen, drawing frantically, trying to hurry up and capture the scene while it was still fresh in my mind. My handiwork did not even come close to what I saw.

CHAPTER 36

. . . .

An Artist Is Born

When we returned home, Rosie and I unpacked our things and settled in. Although I enjoyed my trip, I was eager to see my friends and play some of my favorite music on our little portable record player. Mr. And Mrs. Graves believed in exposing their children to as many opportunities as possible. So when they found out that the neighborhood center was offering a summer arts-and-crafts class for children, they asked if Rosie and I would like to attend. We both agreed to take part in the summer classes. Rosie and I were in separate classes because of our age difference. On my first day, we made paper-mache animals out of paper and paste. I made a dinosaur and named it dinosaur. My teacher said it was the best in the class. Around the third day, we had moved up to finger painting. It was my first time attempting to use paint with my fingers, but it sounded fun. As I was moving the paint around on the paper, the sunset and cactus scene that I saw in Albuquerque came back to my mind. I found myself picking up the tubes of paint that had the colors of the sunset. As I applied the paint to the paper with my fingers, I could see the cactus and the sunset coming to life on my paper. Remembering all the different colors from the desert scene, I tried to do my best to recreate the scene that I saw in the desert. All the other kids were busy painting also. Some of them had their fingers and arms covered in paint, while others had paint all over their clothes. They were just having fun, but I was serious about my painting.

When I finished my painting, I took my painting straight to my teacher. I was so proud of what I had created. She said she could not believe I painted that, but she knew I did it because I was sitting right there in her class. She said it was so good she wanted to put it in a frame and hang it on her wall if I did not mind. I replied, "Yes, please hang it on the wall." I told her, "I am going to paint another one to take home and show my friend Duddy." I painted another one remarkably similar to the first one except the second one had more deep browns, bright oranges, and yellow colors in it. I could hardly wait for class to be over so I could show off my painting to my friend Duddy.

I took my finger painting home, and just as I was entering in the door, Mr. Graves was attempting to walk out the door. We spoke to each other and had a short conversation about my summer class. Then he saw my finger painting in my hand. He asked me what was that in my hand and where I got it from. I explained to him that it was my finger painting and that I just finished painting it in my crafts class. I told him that my teacher liked it so much she hung it on the wall in class. I went on to tell him, "This is the second one I did."

He said, "Let me take a good look at this, Elaine." Then he asked again, "Did you really do this?"

I replied, "Yes, sir, I did it all by myself."

He said, "Oh my goodness, this is beautiful. It looks like the sunset in Albuquerque."

I said with much excitement, "Yes, that is exactly what that is. It got stuck in my head when I saw it on the way home from the trip."

Then Mr. Graves said, "I would like to frame and hang your finger painting in our sitting room."

I said, "Wow, I would be honored for you to hang my painting in our house."

We had a mirror in the sitting room that hung above the desk. Mr. Graves said, "As soon as I get it framed, I am going to replace the mirror with your painting, Elaine. Then everyone who comes in the front door will see your artwork."

I was so happy I felt like crying. Mr. Graves said he believed I had talent. He said the finger painting showed I had the potential to become a good artist. Then out of the clear blue sky, he said he wanted to give me some art lessons to bring out my potential. He added, as soon as he had some free time, he would take me in the basement and give me some lessons. He added that this would also give me a chance to see some of his artwork. I thought, *As good as that sounds, that is not something I want to do with Mr. Graves.* It was not that I was not grateful for his offer, but Mr. Graves was a perfectionist that ran short on patience. I could not imagine him being one of my teachers at school. I truly did not want to be stuck downstairs in the basement with him painting. I could just see him attempting to drive his techniques and style of art down my throat. So I got the bright idea to discourage him from teaching me. I got another sheet of paper and purposely used all kinds of colors that did not complement each other. Then I caused the colors to run together so they would look like I had no idea what I was doing. On completion, it definitely looked like I had no special talent at finger painting. I gave the painting to Mr. Graves the next day, acting so proud of it. I approached him, saying, "Mr. Graves, look what I have done, another painting just for you."

He perked up, all eager to see the painting. He reached and took it from me. Once his eyes fell upon it, he looked surprised and kind of shocked. He asked me, "What is this?"

I replied, "It is a waterfall." But the finger painting had not resembled a waterfall at all.

He poked his lips out as he studied the painting and made a hum sound, as if he were confused. Then he said, "I cannot see a waterfall or anything you are describing in this painting."

I continue to expound on the waterfall.

Mr. Graves said, "Well, Elaine, I guess you were just lucky with those other finger paintings. I think we will just hold off on those art lessons for a little while at least until we find out exactly where your potential is." Then he said, "Maybe when you get in high school, we can look at pursuing those lessons then." And just like that, Mr. Graves never spoke another word to me concerning art lessons.

CHAPTER 37

. . . .

Life Has Its Rewards

After a few weeks back from Albuquerque, our trip was a distant memory. Our social worker named Mrs. Clark stopped by to check on us. We assumed she was making one of her routine checkups, but Mrs. Clark said this was not a routine checkup. She said it was a special visit to show her appreciation to us. She said we had continued to improve dramatically, and out of the twenty-five children assigned to her case load, Rosie and I had grown and improved the most over the past few years. She explained how once a year she would choose a child or two to motivate and encourage by doing something special for them. She continued elaborating on the plans she had made for each of us. She said she was taking us on separate luncheon dates. Mrs. Clark also explained that we needed to wear something appropriate for a classy luncheon. So she said, "Girls, please do not dress like you are going to a fast-food restaurant." Mrs. Clark chose to take me to lunch first. The Stapleton Airport was where she decided to take me. I had never been inside an airport before. There were many times I had passed by wondering what it looked like inside and, on occasion, even sat in the car with Mr. and Mrs. Graves by the landing field, watching the planes take off and land. Mrs. Clark said she wanted me to sit and eat with adults from all walks of life. She believed that by exposing me to businessmen, businesswomen, and wealthy travelers and she felt by exposing me to this kind of environment, it would help me. And I would not be intimidated by anyone when I got older.

The restaurant she took me to was a genuinely nice restaurant. There were mostly white people eating, drinking, and smoking cigarettes. Then I saw one Black female waitress. Mrs. Clark made sure to tell our waitress to seat us by the big window facing the runway and landing field. We could see everything. The planes were taking off and landing like clockwork. I saw one worker loading the plane with bags and another directing the planes to and from the landing field. I could hear on the intercom the flight attendant calling out boarding times and departures. I began to imagine myself rushing to purchase a ticket and boarding the plane going somewhere, anywhere. Mrs. Clark told me to order anything on the menu except wine (in a laughing voice). I began getting nervous because Mrs. Clark was just being too nice to me. I thought there must be something bad that she was planning to tell me and she was just setting me up. The suspense was killing me, so I just came out and asked her so I could stop stressing over it. I asked Mrs. Clark, "Why are we really eating at the airport? Why are you being so nice?"

She could see the fear in my face as I asked that question. She replied, "No, Elaine, there is nothing wrong. As a matter of fact, you are here because I wanted to do something nice for you. Just as I said earlier. And I am going to do the same thing for Rosie, just at a different restaurant. There is no trick or bad news. You are sitting in this room with people who do not look like you but are no different than you. I wanted you to have an opportunity to sit at the table and feel comfortable in the presence of people that are rich and have influential power. You never know where life will lead you, and you should not be intimidated by anyone." She went on to say, "If you continue in school and apply yourself, you can do and have anything in life, just like the people sitting in this restaurant. You girls have been through so much. I am hoping this lunch will play a small part in your success. It is my pleasure to play a role in your healing process as you move into young adulthood and society. I could not imagine contending with all the things you girls have had to deal with. And you turned out to be two beautiful young ladies with unlimited potential. And I want you to continue down that path." Mrs. Clark said, "Elaine, did that answer your question? Or is there anything else that you have concerns about?"

I replied, "No, and I am sorry I had those bad thoughts concerning you." I thought, *What kind of woman is this that she would take that kind of interest in my life? To think about my future to that degree?* I just knew that it was a life-changing lunch. I ordered a T-bone steak, baked potato, salad, and key lime pie from the menu. Then I set up to the table and put my napkin on my lap and begun conversating with Mrs. Clark, laughing, talking, and absorbing all my surroundings while watching the planes take off and land. I got so comfortable it was just as if this was something I did every day. For a moment, I felt like I could be and do anything. I said to myself that the sky was the limit, and this was the world I belonged in. I shared some of my life stories, and Mrs. Clark shared some of hers. But like Cinderella, when the lunch came to an end, the reality set in that I was still a foster child, and there was a long road to travel before I could start thinking about a permanent seat at this kind of table.

CHAPTER 38

. . . .

The Magic Scarf

I could not wait to share my airport experience with my friend Duddy. I went running over to Duddy's house as soon as I got home, but she was not there. Duddy left to attend summer camp. Her mom said she would be gone for a week. I had not made a lot of friends with the other children in the neighborhood, and Rosie had left for the day with her friends. So I just sat on the front porch watching the cars go by, waiting for Rosie to come home to share my awesome lunch with her. While sitting on the front porch, I saw a group of kids walking down the sidewalk. They saw me sitting there on the porch alone. One of them recognized me from my school. It was a guy. He yelled out my name, Elaine. I did not recognize any of those children, but that one looked a little familiar. As they came closer to the porch, I got a better view of them. They came close enough to introduce themselves. The one young man helped me to remember him from the lunchroom. He said his name was Eddie. He asked, "What are you doing sitting here all by yourself?" And I explained that my friend was out of town and my sister was gone with her friends and I had nothing else to do. Eddie said they were looking for somebody's house to go to so they could play their game. He said it's kind of like a magic game. Eddie asked me if I thought it would be okay for them to come in my house and play the game. He said it had to be played indoors. I thought, *What the heck, I am not doing anything else.* I told Eddie, "Let me go ask Mrs. Graves if it would be okay for us to play the game in my bedroom."

Mrs. Graves came to the door and took a look at the kids. She said, "As long as you kids are not jumping around and making a lot of noise, I guess it will be okay."

There was a total of three of them—Eddie, a little girl named Mary, and a little boy named Carl. They were all around my age. I had them follow me up the stairs to my bedroom, where Eddie told us all to have a seat in a circle. And then Eddie pulled out a scarf from under his shirt and said, "This is a magic scarf." It was a scarf that you could wear in the wintertime around your neck. It was kind of thick but not wool.

I asked Eddie, "How do you plan to play a game with just a scarf?"

He said, "You just wait and see. You will be amazed."

We all took a seat on the floor in a circle, and Eddie called for Carl to come sit in the center. Carl took his seat, and Eddie placed the scarf around Carl's neck. He told Carl to take a long breath and hold it. Eddie pulled the scarf tightly on both ends until Carl passed out. I jumped back and said, "Oh, you guys are going to kill him!"

Eddie said, "Just hold on and wait a minute. He will wake up."

We waited about twenty to sixty seconds, and Carl started laughing and kicking while he was still unconscious with his eyes closed. Then suddenly Carl sat straight up and burst out laughing out loud. He said he was experiencing all kinds of tingly things in his hands that were going up and down his arms. He said it felt like little ants running through his body. He started smiling and looking at me and saying, "That was fun. Now it is your turn, Elaine."

I said, "Wait a minute. Let me see Eddie go first."

Eddie said, "Okay, then I will go next, then it is your turn."

I replied, "Okay, that is fine."

Carl put the scarf around Eddie's neck. He took a deep breath and held it while Carl pulled each ends of the scarf tightly until Eddie passed out. He did just like what Carl did except Eddie started acting like he was angry. He looked like he was fussing at somebody. And then he started laughing hysterically and woke up while he was still lying on the floor. As soon as he opened his eyes up and saw me, he said, "Now it is your turn, Elaine. Come sit on the floor. But before we do anything else, let me show you how to signal if the scarf is too tight or if you feel like there is a problem. If your head feels like it is going to burst, do the hand signal. Hold your hand up by your neck and go side to side with your hand moving in a stopping motion, and I will stop." Eddie put the scarf around my neck and pulled the scarf on both ends after I had taken my deep breath. I felt like my head was going to burst. I gave the hand signal for Eddie to stop, and he did. He asked me if I was nervous.

I replied, "Yes, I am."

Eddie said, "You are going to have to relax, or it will not work for you. We'll give you one more try, and if it does not work, we will be done playing the game with you."

I think I started thinking my friends were going to leave me because I could not relax and play the game, and then I was going to be by myself for the rest of the day. So I tried my best to relax and think of things that were nice and fun. And I told Eddie, "I think I am ready."

He put the scarf back around my neck and told me again to take a deep breath and hold it. Once again, Eddie pulled both ends of the scarf tightly. The next thing I knew, I was in a beautiful green field with flowers, and wind was blowing in my face. I saw my favorite dog Lassie running up to me and jumping on me so I could hug and pet him. And then I woke up with these tingly things running up and down my fingers, my hands, and all over my body. They told me I kept calling Lassie, laughing, and smiling before they woke me up. I said to myself I had finally found a game that was free and fun. I just have to learn how to do it by myself. I was doing the magic scarf trick with my friends almost every day after that. We always had to wait until Rosie left the house because Rosie was what we called a square. She would definitely tell if she knew what game we were playing. Eddie and his friends continued to come over almost every day. I started bringing drinks and snacks up to the room, like we were having a little party. Everything was going great until about the sixth day.

It was Mary's turn to go first. We pulled the scarf, just like we always did. Mary fell unconscious with no problems. After about sixty seconds had passed, Mary was not showing any signs of waking up on her own. She started crying while she was unconscious. Eddie said she has been out too long, and we got to get her awake. Eddie tried shaking her to wake her up, but her eyes kept rolling to the back of her head. Eddie said, "Somebody get a cold, wet cloth right now." Luckily, the bathroom was in the next room right outside the door. I grabbed a washcloth and put cold water on it, then handed it to Eddie. He applied it to her face, slapping and tapping her on the face with his hands, trying to get her conscious. Eddie was doing all this, and Mary still was not waking up. That was when Eddie said Mary was having a bad trip and we got to get her awake immediately. He said, "We are going to have to try to get her on her feet."

As Eddie lifted her limp upper body to a sitting position, suddenly Mary jumped to her feet and scared us all half to death. Mary was standing in the middle of the room. We were all leaning back on the floor with our eyes bucked and mouths wide open. Mary said, "Why are you all looking at me that way?" We asked her if she was all right. She replied she was fine other than the tingly filling in her hands and body. It turned out that Mary was okay. We all agreed that was too close for comfort, so we all decided to stop playing the magic scarf game before someone got hurt. The only time I saw Eddie, Mary, or Carl was on this street in passing. We would say our hellos and goodbyes but never spoke of the magic scarf game again.

CHAPTER 39

· · · · · · · · · · · ·

The Fishing Trip

Mrs. Graves informed me and Rosie that we were going on a fishing trip with her and Mr. Graves. We were going to a lake located in the mountains of Golden, Colorado. By now, Rosie and I had become traveling pros. We knew to go to bed early and have our belongings prepared and ready for the long ride ahead. Mrs. Graves informed us that we were spending the night in the camper. Rosie and I went outside to take a look at the camper. It had four pullout beds that looked like bunk beds, a small bathroom, and a kitchen with a table and chairs. After all our chores were done, Rosie and I eagerly went to bed in anticipation of our 2:00 a.m. wake-up call for our first ever fishing trip. After getting a few hours' sleep, we were awakened by Mrs. Graves's voice, yelling, "Girls, it is time to get up." She said, "Roy is loading the car now, and it will not be long before we're on the road." We got up and started gathering our belongings for the trip. Mrs. Graves said, "The campgrounds are in the mountains more than an hour away. So make sure you girls go to the bathroom because we will not be stopping once we're on the road."

When we arrived at the campgrounds, the sun was just peeking above the mountains, reflecting onto the lake. It was so beautiful. There were several campers already parked on the grounds. Each camper was parked next to a picnic table and a firepit for grilling. Once Mr. Graves parked in a designated parking area, we were ready to unload our fishing gear. We all grabbed some fishing supplies and begun setting up our campsite. Mr. Graves had all kinds of fishing supplies in the camper. The first thing I saw him take out of the camper was a small bucket full of worms and little fish called minnows. He used them for bait. He also had a few fishing rods. After a lot of preparation, the time had come for me and Rosie to get our very first fishing lesson. Mr. Graves had bought each of us a bamboo fishing rod. He taught us how to put the bait on the hooks and cast the fishing line into the water. After a few practice times, we were ready to tackle fishing on our own. Mr. Graves changed his clothes and put on some fishing boots, which went all the way up to his thighs. Once he got his fishing reel baited and ready to throw into the water, he slowly walked into the shallow area of the lake and cast his reel. There were a couple of other men standing in the water far off on the other side of the lake. We were the only Black campers that I could see, and Rosie and I were the only children. All the rest of the campers were white males.

It was fun casting my rod at first until I would wait and wait and could not even get a nibble on my fishing line. I would throw my line out, and it would come back just like I threw it out, untouched. Rosie was having much better luck than I was. She had a couple of strong pulls on her line and caught a little bitty fish. Mr. Graves said to throw the little ones back and try for a bigger fish. Rosie threw her line in again and caught a big fish. Mr. Graves was catching fish left and right. He said he had caught a bluegill one minute. The next minute, he said, "Wow, I just caught a trout." Then he said he had another bluegill. I looked around at the other fishermen, and they seemed to be catching a lot of fish also. I continued to try to catch something for a few more hours. I barely got a nibble. I was bored and tired of sitting in the same spot, getting nowhere. I finally gave up and thought it would be a good idea if I went for a walk. Maybe when I returned, there would be a big fish on my line. I asked Mr. Graves if it was okay with him. He laughed and said, "That would be fine, just watch for the rattlesnakes." That was not comforting, hearing about snakes, but for some reason, that did not stop me from wanting to venture off.

As I began my walk toward the other side of the lake, I took time to enjoy looking at the different types of rocks, flowers, and the sunlight shimmering off the blue water reflected by the sky. I was so entranced by the scenic view I did not realize how far I had walked from the campgrounds. I decided that I had probably walked a little too far since I could no longer see the campground. As I turned to go back, I saw what looked to be a cliff at the top of a hill. It was overlooking a portion of the lake. My curiosity led me to venture on to get a good view of the lake. I climbed the small hill and inched my way to the edge of the cliff, making sure to step lightly all the way toward the end of the cliff. Once I reached the tip of the cliff, I stood tall and took in the beautiful view. As I leaned my head forward to get a good peek at some frogs in the water below, suddenly the cliff gave way, and I was thrust down into the murky water. I never learned how to swim or float, so I was afraid I was going to drown. The water was cold and getting into my mouth and nose. I could not see a thing. It was pitch black. That was probably because I had my eyes closed, panicking. I was under the water, and then I surfaced to the top. I was yelling, flapping my arms, and kicking. I was bobbing up and down, yelling, "Help! Help! I am drowning." I continued yelling, "Somebody, please help me!" I started swallowing that nasty water every time I yelled for help and started going under again. By now my imagination was taking over because all I could think about was getting bit by a snake and drowning at the same time. I saw some roots protruding out from the sides of the lake. I tried to grab ahold to one of the roots to pull myself out or at least hold on until help could come, but the roots were too slippery. Because I had walked so far from the campground, no one could hear me.

Just as I was going down for the third time, a nearby white man heard my cries for help. He came running and jumped in the lake and pulled me out. He saved my life. He was about six feet tall and had big muscles, a beard, and kind eyes. My hero made sure I was okay, and then he carried my dripping wet body back to our campsite. As we approached the campground, Mr. and Mrs. Graves saw me in the arms of a stranger, drenching wet. They dropped what they were doing and ran up to us, saying, "Oh my god, what happened?"

Rosie dropped her fishing rod and came running also. They were all asking what happened and if I was all right. My hero, the white man, answered and said, "She's okay. She is just shaken up from almost drowning. All she needs now are some dry clothes and a little comforting, and she will be fine." Mr. and Mrs. Graves were so thankful for the man saving my life. They repeatedly tried to offer him some type of compensation for his heroic deed, but he refused any type of reward. He told Mr. and Mrs. Graves that he had to get back to his fishing but to please be sure to get me some swimming lessons. And then as fast as he came into my life, he was gone.

Mrs. Graves took me inside the camper to get me out of the wet clothing. She had me wrap up in a big, thick blanket as she rinsed my clothes and hung them up to dry. She made a homemade clothesline out of a fishing line and two tree branches. Then she made me a cup of hot tea to sip on while my clothes hung on the line to dry. I was surprised I did not get yelled at. I guessed they were so happy that I did not drown. They did not care how it happened.

As it began to get dark, Mr. Graves made a campfire for Mrs. Graves to cook on. Mrs. Graves was busy cleaning and scaling the fish Mr. Graves had caught. She had prepared the fish with a corn-meal batter. She put the skillet on the fire and added some cooking oil and then put the fish into the hot skillet. Mrs. Graves yelled out, "Girls, would you like to roast a couple of hot dogs when I finish frying the fish?"

Rosie and I both shouted out, "Yes!"

Mr. Graves told us to pick out a couple of good tree branches to use to cook the hot dogs. He said, "Make sure they're not too thick or not too skinny." We gathered our branches and gave them to Mr. Graves. He used his hunting knife to cut away the outer bark, and then he used his knife to make two points, one on each end of the sticks. He stuck the hot dogs firmly on one end of the stick, then handed the sticks to each of us. Mr. Graves said we could use the same sticks later for roasting marshmallows if we wanted to. As soon as Mrs. Graves was finished cooking, Rosie and I sat in front of the fire, roasting our hot dogs. I was still wrapped in the blanket. This reminded me of something I had seen in an old Western movie.

Just as I went to bite into my hot dog, Mrs. Graves said, "Not so fast, we are still eating with our manners." She pulled out some plastic plates and forks. She said, "I also brought salad to go with the fish." She cooked all the varieties of fish that Mr. Graves and Rosie had caught. That was the first time I had ever had food cooked on a campfire, and it was so good. At the end of our meal, Mrs. Graves said it was time for dessert and pulled out a bag of marshmallows. She said, "We are getting ready to have some fun roasting marshmallows, girls." We put our marshmallows on our sticks and sat and roasted marshmallows over the campfire with the Graves. That was one of the best nights in my life. I promised myself that I would always remember that day. I knew it was rare for Black children in those days to be at a campground roasting marshmallows, cooking hot dogs, and cooking fish we caught and cleaned right at the site. And to top it off, I had been saved by a stranger from drowning all in one day. I thanked God for that day and my foster family. The next morning, we packed up everything and headed back home.

CHAPTER 40

. . . .

The Amusement Park

Life was getting better and better with the Graves. The next week, Mrs. Graves said she wanted to take us to an amusement park. I had been told Denver had a couple of real nice ones. One was named Lakeside; the other was Elitch Gardens. I had never been to an amusement park before, so I had no idea what to expect. On the day of the event, Mrs. Graves told us to dress up in one of our nice pantsuits. She said she was going to be wearing a short-sleeve summer dress and a light jacket to keep her from getting sun-burnt. She chose Lakeside to be the first amusement park for us to attend. Mrs. Graves still did not know how to drive, so the public city bus was our means of transportation. The bus ride was fun. We got a chance to see parts of Denver we had never seen before. After about a thirty-minute ride, the bus let us off right in front of Lakeside. We could see that the amusement park was huge. We walked right up to the entrance, and Mrs. Graves purchased our tickets, and we walked inside. This amusement park had everything—from a gigantic roller coaster, a laughing lady at the top of the fun house, wheelbarrows that would spin as you walked through them, to all types of food. Lakeside also had something really different located in the lake. It was hundreds of catfish around the bridge. You could walk over and feed the catfish. The catfish piled on top of one another, poking their mouths up in the air and trying to get some popcorn or whatever you threw in the water. Lakeside was an amazing, exciting, and beautiful place to attend.

Rosie and I wore Mrs. Graves out. We were going from one ride to another. Our first rides were the Octopus, Wild Chipmunk, and the roller coaster named the Cyclone. There were so many different rides. Mrs. Graves said she had never walked so much in her life. And the next time we went, she planned to stay home. Nevertheless, we continued to enjoy ourselves way into the evening hours, eating some of the best hamburgers and fries that I had ever tasted. At nightfall, the whole place lit up with beautiful lights, like a wonderland. It was another awesome experience with Mrs. Graves. At closing time, we got on the bus with all our souvenirs and good memories and headed back home without any incidents. Life was good for me and Rosie. In those days, we continued to go on fishing and camping trips. We even had a chance to go to Mr. Graves's family reunion.

We attended Mr. Graves's family reunion in Columbia, Missouri, for a weekend. The family reunion was fun and educational. There were lots of food, games, and backyard parties for the kids and adults. They had daytime and nighttime parties. It was at the family reunion where I saw my first lightning bug. I could hardly believe what I was seeing when I saw the first lighting bug in a tree. First, there was one light blinking in the tree. Then all of a sudden, the whole tree was lit up. The trees were beautifully lit up with all the different colors. There was red, yellow, and orange lightning bugs in the trees. And then we were surrounded with lightning bugs. They were no longer in the trees. They were flying and landing on everything. One landed on my pants. I quickly grabbed and put it in my pocket. Once I realized they did not fly fast, I was able to catch them. I grabbed as many lights as possible and put them all in my pockets. The next morning, to my surprise, all I had was a pocketful of black bugs, no lights. I guess that was why they were named lightning bugs, not flying lights.

The family reunion turned out to be a lot of fun, and the time went so fast. The weekend was over, and it was time to head back home. The next day, on the drive back, we noticed Mr. and Mrs. Graves kept having arguments about one thing or another. We could tell something was definitely wrong. We figured something must have happened in Columbia, Missouri, at one of the parties because their relationship was not the same after the family reunion. They hardly had two words to say to each other. After we returned home, they began to argue on and off. There was a lot of tension in the house.

CHAPTER 41

. . . .

The Other Side of Mr. Graves

When we got back from Columbia, Missouri, everything seemed to start changing. Mr. Graves started staying out late at night, not coming home from work. Instead, he was coming in around 11:00 p.m. and 12 a.m. He started missing dinner altogether, and that was not like him. And then one night, around two in the morning, I was awakened to hear some fussing downstairs. I tried to wake Rosie up so we could go see what was going on. I could not get Rosie to wake up, so I tiptoed down the stairs by myself to the entrance of the basement door. I carefully poked my head around the corner of the staircase just enough to see what was going on, trying to be careful enough not to allow them to see me. I saw Mr. Graves hit Mrs. Graves on her arms and back. It scared me so bad. I started crying and ran back upstairs. I jumped back in my bed and threw the cover over my head. Seeing him hit her caused me to have a flashback of when my mother was getting beat in the bathtub. After I got back in the bed, I could still hear Mrs. Graves crying. As he continued yelling at her, I just lay in my bed and cried myself to sleep.

When I awoke the next morning, I was trying to tell Rosie what had happened and what I saw. Rosie tried to tell me I was probably having a nightmare because she did not hear anything. She was about to convince me that maybe it was just a bad dream. So I got my clothes on and ventured downstairs to the kitchen. I needed to see for myself if I was dreaming or not. As I approached Mrs. Graves,

I was looking to see if she had any marks on her. As I entered the kitchen, I said, "Good morning." She did not reply at first. I said "Good morning" again, and she replied in a low-tone voice, "Good morning." She did not seem to be her regular, happy self. As a matter of fact, she did not look happy at all. I walked around to the front of her and looked at her arms. She had a big black and blue bruise on her upper arm and another big black bruise on her leg. I asked her if she was okay, and she replied yes. When she saw me looking at her bruises, she told me to run along until she called us for breakfast. She said she had a lot on her mind right now. She gave me a look like "Please do not ask me any more questions." She had a look of helplessness on her face. I felt so sad for her, and I began to fear Mr. Graves. I said to myself, if he would do that to her, he would do that to me.

After that, I started waking up in the middle of the night to see if he continued abusing her, but I never heard them fight again. The next week, Mr. Graves's son named Ronald Graves and his wife, named Laura, moved in with us. They took residence in the spare bedroom next to our bedroom. Ronald had just finished college, and so did his wife. They were looking to stay with Mr. and Mrs. Graves until they could buy their first home. They had just relocated from North Carolina. Ronald was looking for a job as a pharmaceutical sales representative. His wife, Laura, was in the educational field. She was looking for work as an administrator. Ronald was reserved and highly intelligent, but he had a sense of humor that made me enjoy being around him. Once Ronald got to know me and Rosie, he became more like our big brother. He would give us advice on different topics and continually reminded us to make sure to get a good education and stay away from bad boys. His wife, Laura, stayed to herself in their room most of the time. I never had a meaningful conversation with her nor did Rosie. I noticed Ronald and Mr. Graves were not talking much anymore. I did not know if the stress from Ronald and Laura living in the house was getting to Mr. Graves or if he was just still having problems from Columbia, Missouri. After about three months, Ronald and his wife found work and moved out.

Mr. Graves started coming in later and later, around two thirty-three in the morning on weekends. And his disposition seemed to be angry and impatient all the time. One night, Mr. Graves came in late, around 3:00 a.m. He went to the kitchen and got a glass out of the cabinet. He saw some water spots on the glass. He got so angry when he saw those spots on the glass. He started yelling and screaming for me and Rosie to come downstairs and look at the glass. We were awakened out of a dead sleep by him yelling our names. We jumped up and went down the stairs in our pajamas, wondering what was going on. When we reached the kitchen, Mr. Graves was standing there with a glass in his hand. He was shaking it at us, saying, "Look at this glass. Do you see what I see? There are spots on this glass." He repeated, "There are water spots on this glass." I had no idea what he was talking about. We had been washing dishes earlier that day in the dishwasher. Occasionally, some glasses would have water spots, but Rosie and I would normally wipe down all glasses, dishes, and silverware with a dishcloth, making sure to remove all spots before putting them away. "So we missed one or two, but there cannot be many more," I said to myself.

Mr. Graves grabbed both me and Rosie by our arms and pulled us over to the sink in front of the kitchen cabinets, where the glasses were stored. He opened up the kitchen cabinet and took out another glass and said, "I see another water spot." He yelled out, "If you are going to do something, do it right the first time, and you will not have to do it a second time." Then he said, "Since you girls failed to do it right the first time, I am going to teach you a lesson." He pulled out all the silverware drawer and turn it upside down in the kitchen sink. Then he pulled out another drawer, dumping all the large cooking utensils into the sink, and he instructed us to rewash every glass in the cabinet and every piece of silverware in the sink. Then he said, "When you are finished, place everything back in its proper place." He told us, if he found one spot on anything in the morning, we would be put on punishment for the next two weeks. Rosie and I washed all the dishes, glasses, and silverware until the sun came up, making sure not to leave a spot on anything and putting everything back in its proper place. The next morning, Mr. Graves told us everything looked good, and he hoped we learned our lesson. I answered, "Yes, sir," but Rosie did not say anything. He told us we were okay to leave the house and gave us our $10 weekly allowance.

About two weeks later, Mr. Graves came home in the middle of the night and woke us up again except this time, he wanted to ask us questions about our grades in school. He wanted us to give him information on every class we were taking at 2:30 a.m. I was so nervous I could hardly think what classes I was taking or what my grades were. Rosie and I were both half asleep as he drilled us on our school activities. He started asking us to solve math problems. I could not believe he was doing this to us for no reason. Here we were standing in the kitchen in our pajamas around two thirty in the morning, trying to do a math calculation. He was throwing out decimals, fractions, and whatever type of calculation he could come up with. Rosie was good in math. She had no problem answering when he called her out. On the other hand, I was not that good in math, and I would freeze up when he called on me. I would just go blank in my mind. I was so afraid that I might give the wrong answer I could not think. Fortunately, this particular night, he was tired, and whatever answer I gave satisfied him. After all the questionings were done, he told me and Rosie to get some ice cream and go back to bed. I did not know what made him stop, but after that night, he did not call on us to get up out of our sleep for any reason anymore.

All that anger Mr. Graves had must have been rubbing off on me and Rosie because we began to argue more and more. It seemed like I was tired of her and she was tired of me. About a month later, we got in an argument over nothing of importance, just disagreeing with each other's opinion. Rosie started twisting my arm behind my back, threatening to break my arm. Rosie was strong, and I was trying to work myself loose from her grip, but she kept twisting my arm tighter and tighter to the point that I thought she was going to break it. I decided to do something to make her turn me loose, so I bit down onto her arm and locked my teeth in her arm, like a pit bull. All I remembered after that was her fist up my head. Rosie hit me so hard she knocked me unconscious. I fell down a flight of stairs. I hit the stairs so hard it made a loud *boom, bam, boom* sound that scared Mrs. Graves half to death. She came running, yelling, "Girls, what is going on? Stop that fighting right this minute." I was down at the bottom of the stairs all twisted up, trying to wake up from being knocked unconscious. When I came to, I tried to tell Mrs. Graves that Rosie was twisting my arm for no reason. I had not done anything to her. I had no other choice but to bite her to keep her from breaking my arm. But Rosie was Mrs. Graves's favorite child, and when Rosie showed Mrs. Graves my teeth prints I left on her arm, Mrs. Graves said that we were both wrong. She said she would put us both on punishment if we did not stop. I never thought Mrs. Graves liked me as much as Rosie, and this incident confirmed my thinking. I was upset with both of them.

CHAPTER 42

. . . .

Earth, Wind, and Fire

This was when Rosie and I started going in our own direction. Rosie and I had started drinking alcohol from Mr. Graves's fully stocked bar in the dining room. We would replace the clear liquor with water. Most of the liquor we took was gin, vodka, or tequila. We would take the liquor to the park and drink it, or sometimes we would drink it at school. Rosie started drinking a lot more than I did. I was actually thinking about starting back using the scarf. I started going to parties further and further from home. Most were late-night parties down by the Five Points area. I looked older for my age and always knew someone at the house parties that would lie and say I was sixteen when in reality I was around eleven years old. The house parties never served liquor, but they still wanted you to be at least sixteen.

Meanwhile, my second to the oldest sister Oma and her husband, named Clifton, had moved in our neighborhood. Their house was located only a few blocks from ours on Gaylord Street. They had a nice brick house with a front porch, like Mr. and Mrs. Graves had. Their house had three bedrooms and a basement. You could sit in their front room and look straight out their picture window and see the beautiful snowcapped mountain called Pikes Peak. Oma's husband, Clifton, told me that one of his famous friends lived in the neighborhood on the other side of the block. Clifton said his friend belonged to a group called Earth, Wind, and Fire. He said he was going to show me where his house was, and if the opportunity aRosie, he would introduce me to one of the singers. I was elated when my uncle Clifton told me that. I said he was the best uncle ever.

I listened to the music of Earth, Wind, and Fire all the time. I already had a couple of their forty-five records at home. I found myself going over Oma and Clifton's house every chance I got, hoping it would be a good day for Clifton to introduce me to his Earth, Wind, and Fire friend. Listening to music was one of the things that enabled me to cope with life. Earth, Wind, and Fire was one of the hottest groups in America at that time. Once the word got out that one of the singers lived by my sister and brother-in-law, my friends and I would sometimes just walk by the house, hoping to get a glimpse of one of the recording artists, but we never saw anyone enter or leave the house. My uncle Clifton told me they had to start entering through their back alley because their privacy was being invaded, and now was not a good time to try to meet them. I never got to see any of them, so I settled with just the idea of knowing that I stood in front of the home that the great Earth, Wind, and Fire practiced in.

CHAPTER 43

. . . .

Visiting Mom in Pueblo

Mrs. Graves said our grandmother had called and said she was planning a family trip to Pueblo to see our mother. She said we would be leaving and returning all in the same day. I was so happy to know I was going to be able to see my mother. I had really missed seeing her. No matter what she did to get herself institutionalize, she was still my mother, and I still loved her. That following Saturday, my grandmother came and picked me and Rosie up. Raney was already in the car. Oma could not go for some reason unknown to me. Lena had already moved to California to live with her dad. DD had gotten adopted by my aunt Connie and moved to California. My grandfather drove the station wagon. My grandmother sat in the front passenger seat. Raney and Rosie sat in the second seat, and I sat on the last row of the station wagon with a lot of bags and boxes. Gran had packed all kinds of food and drinks. They were all neatly packed in the rear on the flatbed of the station wagon. Gran had no problem serving up the snacks once we were on the road. It was a long, boring ride once we got past Colorado Springs. There was nothing to see, just flat land. My grandmother did not believe in children playing cards, so we had to be careful what games we played around my grandmother, as Christian children.

After several hours, we finally reached Pueblo. The first thing I noticed was there were no tall buildings that resembled a downtown area, only a few restaurants and small store fronts. It definitely was nothing like Denver. Then we reached the hospital. It was a huge building that looked like something out of an old movie. It was so big it looked more like it should have been a prison, anything other than a hospital. As my grandfather pulled into a parking area, my grandmother started instructing us how to carry ourselves once we entered the facility. She said, "Do not talk to any of the patients other than your mom or stare or laugh at them in any way." She explained that some of the patients did not look sick at all, while others patients looked extremely ill. Gran said, "If all goes well inside with your mom, we will be allowed to take her outside and have our picnic on the front lawn." As we approached the entrance, a nurse came to the door and escorted us into a waiting area. We were told to have a seat while my mother was being prepared to come and join us. We were sitting in the general seating area. There was a TV and several round tables with chairs. All the staff was dressed in white. Even the men had white pants, white shirts, and white shoes, and the nurses had on little white hats, which matched their white uniforms.

As we continued to sit for almost twenty minutes while waiting on our mother to be escorted to the sitting room, I saw a man standing in the corner bumping his head against the wall. In another corner, I saw a lady arguing and fussing with herself as though there was someone standing there that she was talking to. Another man was sitting in a chair just staring at me as if he had never seen a little Black girl before. I was just about to get frustrated with the time it was taking for them to bring my mom out when I saw my mother walking down a long hallway with a nurse walking beside her. As soon as my mom entered the waiting room, I jumped up and ran to her and gave her a big hug. She smiled and said, "Laney, I sure did miss your hugs." Then Rosie, Oma, Raney, and my grandparents all got around her and were hugging her as the other patients looked on in amazement or jealousy.

The nurse said, "It looks like everything is going fine, so you all are allowed to go outside and have your picnic on the front lawn, as you requested." There was a designated area where patients could have fellowship with their families inside a gated area. There were a couple of tables and chairs, but my grandmother wanted to sit on the grass. She brought two big blankets for us to sit on. While my grandmother was spreading out the blankets, my grandfather went to the car to get the picnic baskets. Upon his return with the picnic baskets, we all had a seat on the blankets. Gran told us all to join hands, and my grandmother prayed right there on the hospital grounds. Gran handed out pops, potato chips, sandwiches, and cookies. There was not a cloud in the sky, and the temperature was perfect.

I lay on my back on the blanket and just looked at my mom, then I looked at that huge building. I said to myself, "What are they doing to her in there?" because the other people in the sitting room did not look happy at all. I wondered how many days my mom looked like the other patients. I asked my mom how she was doing in the building. She responded, "Your mom is trying to get adjusted to her medication. It seems to be working after a lot of different trials." She said, "I think I am on the right medication to the point I believe I will be getting out the hospital soon."

That was great news to hear. No one had told me she was getting close to being released from the hospital. We stayed on the hospital grounds for a couple hours before a nurse came out and said it was time for my mom to go back inside and visiting hours were over. We had to gather our things and prepared to leave. I knew it was hard on my grandmother, but she never complained, not once. She was doing a great job keeping the family together. Gran was always positive, encouraging, and trusting in the Lord for everything. When we finished gathering our things and loading the car, we gave our hugs and goodbye kisses to my mom as we all walked back to the sitting room. We all watched my mom return to her room as the nurse escorted her back down that long hallway. Then we all exited the room and headed back to the car. On the drive back, we all took turns sharing and discussing how we enjoyed our mom and how we were adapting to our different foster homes. Gran and Papa returned us to our foster homes, where we said our goodbyes and gave our hugs and kisses until we could meet again.

CHAPTER 44

. . . .

Coors Beer Trip

When we got back home, Mr. Graves seemed to be in a better mood. I thought maybe he missed us. He announced that he wanted to take us to the Coors beer brewery in Colorado Springs. He said we still had a week before school started, so we could fit one more trip in. He asked Rosie what she thought and if she would like to go. At first, we thought it was a trick question since Rosie and I had been taking his liquor and replacing it with water, but it was not a trick question, and we said yes. That next Saturday, Mr. And Mrs. Graves loaded up the car with snacks and drinks. Then off to Colorado Springs we went. The trip to Colorado Springs seemed short after the long trip to Pueblo. Plus, Colorado Springs was absolutely gorgeous. We had all the beautiful snowcapped mountains surrounding us, including my favorite one, named Pikes Peak.

Once we reached the Coors beer brewery, it was huge. As we entered into the facility, I saw a fountain of water. People were dipping a ladle in the water to get a cup of the crystal-clear spring water. I thought that was so creative. I had to get a cup of that water for myself. We were assigned a tour guide, and he said the fountain was our first stop. Oh, my goodness, that water was so good. It was the best water I ever tasted in my life. I thought, *I wonder what that beer tastes like?* Needless to say, no children were allowed to sample any beer. Mr. Graves was having a good old time drinking lots of beer. He said it was free as long as he drank the samples. We had an opportunity to tour the brewery with our tour guide. We saw the big containers the hops were stored in and how the beer was brewed and bottled. Mr. Graves seemed so happy on that day. It reminded me of how happy he used to be before we went to Columbia, Missouri.

Before our tour was over, we got a chance to smell and touch the hops that were used in making the beer. The tour guide was genuinely nice and informative. It was an educational experience as well as enjoyable. At the end of the tour, Mrs. Graves, Rosie, and I all bought ourselves some souvenirs. Mr. Graves bought a few cases of that freshly brewed beer for himself. We thanked all the people at Coors who helped make our trip a success. And we headed back home after having another wonderful experience with Mr. and Mrs. Graves.

CHAPTER 45

. . . .

School and Mom

We had finally reached the week before school registration. Mrs. Graves had given us plenty of money to complete our back-to-school wardrobe. One of my favorite pieces I bought for my first day was a tight olive-green two-piece skirt and jacket. It was made out of polished cotton with four gold buttons going down the front. Rosie and I both dressed very conservatively and preppy. We always looked like little secretaries, as if we were working in an office. One of my favorite styles of dressing came from a TV mom by the name of Mrs. Cleaver. She was the mother on the *Leave It to Beaver* sit-com show. I loved her wardrobe choices, and occasionally, she would wear a tight-fitting dress that complemented her figure. She always dressed well for her husband, and that mattered a lot to me since my life's goal was to get married. The show gave me an example of a husband and a family that I wanted to be like. It did not matter to me that they were white. I was sure I would have chosen a Black family if there were any black families on TV at that time.

The first day of school finally came, and my best friend Duddy stopped by to join me and Rosie on our walk to school. Cole Junior High was a large interracial school located on Thirty-Fourth and Humboldt about a mile from our house. It did not take me long to make friends with the children that had such diverse backgrounds. I loved to talk to all the students and learn about their culture and their different lifestyles. When I returned home, Mrs. Graves had some good news for me and Rosie. She said that our mom had just been released from the hospital on a probational period. Her doctors wanted to see if she could adjust to living in an apartment on her own, and if she did well, she would be permanently released from the state institution. I got my mom's address, which was located in northeast Denver. I caught a public transportation bus and immediately went to visit her. She was living in an old redbrick apartment building close to the Five Points area in northeast Denver. When I knocked on the door, an older white lady answered, she introduced herself as Mrs. Gills. She said she was the caretaker of the boarding house and explained the visiting rules to me. She went on to say there were six other tenants living in the building, and everyone shared the same bathroom, kitchen, and living room area. Then Mrs. Gills told me my mom's room number and pointed to the hallway that led upstairs to my mom's bedroom. Once I reached the top of the stairs, I saw a man sitting on the side of his bed listening to the radio in his room. My mom's room was next to his room.

When I knocked on her door, she asked who it was. When she heard my voice, she got so excited and ran and opened the door and hugged me so tightly she almost picked me up off the floor. I never saw my mother that happy to see someone. I thought she must have gotten a breakthrough in the hospital because she was totally different. She sat on her full-size bed. I sat in a worn-out dark-green chair next to a small window. The window was facing the side of another old brick building. She also had a dark-brown dresser with a mirror. Mom started talking about her plans to get a house and get all her girls out of foster care. I knew she was not in shape to get us out of foster care, but it was really nice listening to her desires. I was able to share some of my school experiences with her. After a few hours had passed, my visiting hours were coming to an end. Talking and listening to my mom on that day was like my mom and I were in a penthouse suite with an oceanside view. We were so happy.

When it was time to go, my mom wanted to show me around the apartment building. She was proud to introduce me to a few of the tenants. They were sitting in the living room as we walked through, and then we took a quick peek into the large kitchen. I saw a big table and chairs in the center of the room and all the appliances, like a stove, a fridge, and a sink. From there we walked through the hall, and I exited the apartment building. As my mom stood at the front door, waving goodbye, I thought God was really good. I thought my mom was on the road to recovery after all these years. She continued to work hard, getting herself prepared for her new start in life. After about six months, she was allowed to move out of the seven-tenant boarding house and into her very own apartment.

Once I found out my mom had moved to a new location, I caught the city bus to the house that my mom was renting. The house was located in southeast Denver on Lawrence Street. This type of house was called a shotgun house. It got its name from being long and narrow. When my mom answered the door, the first thing I noticed was her stomach. She looked like she was pregnant again. I said, "Wow, Mom, you look like you're pregnant again!"

She answered, "Yes, Lane, and this time, I know it is a boy."

I thought, *Oh no, here she goes again, hoping for that boy.*

After listening to her go on about her pregnancy, she said, "I want you to meet Lubert, my boyfriend and the baby's daddy." She said, "His name is Lubert, and he is asleep, but I am going to wake him up so he can meet you." She walked me straight back to the first bedroom. Mom woke him up, and he sat up on the edge of the bed. She introduced me to him and said, "This is Lane, one of my daughters."

He was trying to be friendly and pleasant, considering he was awakened out of a deep sleep. I was shocked when the cover came off his legs. I saw he only had one leg. I had never seen a man up close with one leg. Lubert noticed that I was staring at his amputated leg and took the initiative to help me get over the fear of seeing an amputee. He called me over to his side and told me how he lost his leg in a car accident and then pointed to his artificial leg that was propped up over in the corner. He asked me if I could help him by handing him his leg. At first, I was going to say no, but my mom was looking on, and I did not want her to feel like I was afraid of her boyfriend. Then he said, "It will not bite you. Just pick it up like a toy and hand it to me." He smiled, and I smiled back and picked up his heavy leg and handed it to him. After that, I was no longer afraid of his amputation or his artificial leg. I found Lubert to actually be a nice man, and he seemed like he made my mother happy. That was all that I ever wanted, a man who would make my mom happy. I did not care if he did not have any legs or arms. If he could make my mom happy, I was happy.

My mom called me into the kitchen. She was talking about my baby sister DD and talking about the pajamas that she had bought for DD because she was planning to bring her home for a while. She continued sharing her hopes and dreams to get all her children out of foster homes and back with her when she got a bigger place. She was sharing her bit of wisdom, trying to explain to me to stay focused and stay in school. Then she said, "Do your absolute best to stay out of trouble." I enjoyed that day talking and laughing with my mom and Lubert. It brought back so many memories of the days when our lives were just peaceful and simple before the horrible incident in the projects. We talked until it began to get dark. She told me to promise her I would do my best to get a good education and stay out of trouble. I promised her and then gave her a kiss and Lubert a big hug, and I left.

CHAPTER 46

. . . .

Church, It's Not What
It Looks Like

On my way home, I thought about what my mother said, about being good and especially staying out of trouble. And coincidentally that day, Mrs. Graves told me and Rosie that we should start going to church. She said there was a Baptist church close by that we could attend, or we could choose another one of our choice, but we needed to go to church somewhere. Rosie and I chose the First Baptist Church that was a few blocks from our school. Rosie and I both agreed that we would go, and if we liked it, we would become members. That following Sunday, we went to First Baptist Church, and surprisingly, we enjoyed the service. It was the first time I actually understood what a preacher was saying. His sermon was about charity, helping your fellow man or woman. Helping those who were less fortunate than you was what he tried to convey to his congregation. At the end of church, while the choir was singing, Rosie and I discussed the sermon, and we both agreed it was a really good message. After our discussion, while church service was going on, they gave the benediction and asked if anyone would like to join the church. Rosie and I both agreed we wanted to be part of this church, and we went down to the altar, and we joined right there on the spot. They asked if we wanted to get baptized, and we both agreed that yes, we wanted to be baptized. They gave us a date and a time that they would be having baptisms. We agreed that we would come back to be baptized on that day. They gave us each a Bible and told us to take it home and study the word of God.

Rosie and I were so moved by the message, friendly people, and the word of God. On our way home, RRosie and I were singing the gospel song and feeling blessed. We both talked about how life had changed for us, and we were living like rich kids compared to a lot of other children. We even discussed giving some of our allowance to some of the children that were less fortunate. During all this loving talk of charity, we stumbled up on a man sitting on the curb. He looked like he could be about nineteen years old. He had a uniform on and a duffel bag at his side, looking destitute. Rosie looked at me, and I looked at her, and we both said at the same time, "Are you thinking what I am thinking?" And we both said yes. Then we asked the man sitting on the curb if he needed some help and why he was sitting on the curb.

He looked at us strangely and said, "Who are you, and why do you care?"

So I told the man, "This is my sister, Rosie, and my name is Elaine. We just left church, and we heard the message that was preached about charity and helping our sisters and brothers that are less fortunate. We are asking you because we want to know, do you need help, and if you do, how can we help you?"

This stranger said his name was Todd, and he had just gotten back from Vietnam. That was when Rosie and I got the bright idea to offer Todd food and shelter for the night. We told Todd if he would like to, he could come home with us. We could sneak him into our bedroom, and he could get a good night's rest that might help him to think a little clearer to be able to apply for a job. Todd said, "I cannot believe my ears." He asked us, "Are you offering me a place to spend the night?"

We said. "Yes, that is exactly what we are doing." I said, "We have more than enough food for you, and we have two bunk beds. You can sleep on the lower bunk, and Rosie and I will sleep on the top bunk."

He said it sounded good to him, but were we sure it would be all right with our parents? I thought, *This man is homeless and has nowhere to go. Isn't this what the church was just talking about?* Rosie and I looked at each other again and said, "You're going to go with us."

Todd said, "Are you sure that is going to be okay with your parents?"

I replied, "No, they cannot know you are in the house. We will have to sneak you up through our bedroom window, and you will have to climb the tree onto the roof and into the bedroom window." I added, "But it is not hard to do because I do it all the time when I sneak out to go to parties, and I'd never been caught."

He said, "Well, it sounds okay with me, then, if you are sure it will not get you in trouble."

We said, "Somebody has got to help you, and we can help."

Todd was a young Black man about five feet three inches tall and around 130 pounds, not much bigger than me and Rosie. He seemed to be a kind person at heart and was just down on his luck, and getting fresh out the military did not help him. We all worked together carrying his bags to the house. Our plan worked perfectly. We snuck Todd in the backyard up the tree and onto the roof. We got him through the window in broad daylight. We helped Todd with getting his duffel bag and his shoulder bag into the house. Once we got Todd in the house, we gave him a washcloth and a little pan of water to allow him to freshen up. We turned our backs to give him some privacy while he put on our pajamas. Once we got him all squared away into our pajamas, we made him a couple of turkey sandwiches with potato chips and a pop. Rosie and I were eager to teach him how to play a game of old maid. We acted like we had a brand-new brother. We were both trying to show and tell him all about the new games we had. Todd was careful not to laugh or talk too loud, but we made sure to keep the record player playing the whole time to drown out the sound of his voice. Mrs. Graves never came into the room without knocking first. She always talked about how you should always knock before entering a room even if it was inside the house, and she always did that. That was one reason Rosie and I thought we could pull this off so easily. Our plan was, once she knocked on the door, Todd was to dive onto the bed and get under the covers, and Rosie or I would answer the door. It sounded pretty simple and easy to do. What could go wrong with something that simple?

We played Monopoly and Candy Land and old maid card games until almost eleven o'clock at night. We were having a wonderful time with Todd. The plan was, in about thirty more minutes, we were all going to say a prayer, then get some sleep. Another thing RRosie and I were not worried about was any type of molestation from Todd because we were both virgins, and that was not on our minds. Rosie had just made the decision. It had gotten late, and we all needed to get some rest, and we put away the games. As fate would have it, as soon as Todd got up to help hand the Monopoly board to Rosie, Mrs. Graves walked in the door without knocking. She was holding two beautiful banana splits in her hand. She had a big smile on her face that quickly turned to fear. It looked like time stood still for a few seconds. Rosie and I stopped in our tracks and took a deep breath, frozen with our eyes bucked looking at her. Todd was handing Rosie the game. He just dropped it and froze in place, as if that was going to make him invisible. All our eyes were bucked, and our mouths were open in shock. Rosie and I were just as shocked that Mrs. Graves came in without knocking as she was to see a man standing in our bedroom. She just stood there for about seven seconds, trying to understand what her eyes were seeing. Still holding those banana splits in her hands, once she processed in her mind that Todd was a man and he had on our pajamas in our bedroom, she was left with one conclusion, and it was not good.

That was when things got ugly. Mrs. Graves screamed to the top of her voice, "Oh my God! There is a man in the house!" And she continued yelling, "Roy (Roy was Mr. Graves's first name), come quick! The girls have a man in their bedroom." Before we could say anything, Mrs. Graves turned to run out the room and said, "You girls have really done it now." We tried to stop her from running out the room by explaining that we were just trying to help Todd in his time of need, like the church said.

I yelled out, "Mrs. Graves, please wait! It is not what it looks like!" Mrs. Graves did not want to hear anything I had to say and continued to run downstairs to get Mr. Graves. When Mr. Graves started running up the stairs, we could hear his feet on the staircase getting closer and closer. Rosie and I were in panic mode right now. We started yelling at Todd, "Get out those pajamas and jump out the window! We will throw your bag down to you." Todd was in shock. He was not moving extremely fast. I said, "Todd, hurry! Quick, you got to get out the window now." Todd was trying to put his other leg into his pants, but he still had our pajama top on.

By now Mr. Graves had reached our bedroom door. At first, he did what Mrs. Graves did and stood there in shock or disbelief for a few seconds, seeing Todd standing there with our pajama top half on and half off. Mr. Graves lost it. He went into a full-on panic mode. He started swearing and saying he was going to kill Todd. Todd thought if he tried to explain the situation, it would help. So Todd said, "Sir, they were just trying to help me. They were not doing anything bad. I am so sorry for causing a problem."

Mr. Graves said, "I know you are sorry. So you just stay right there because I am going to kill you." Mr. Graves turned and ran through the hall and down the stairs to get his rifle in the hall closet. The whole time he was running, he was yelling, "I am going to kill you for coming up in my house!"

Rosie and I were really yelling now, saying, "Todd, jump out the window and run as fast as you can."

Mr. Graves was yelling on his way down the stairs, saying, "I will teach you a lesson. I do not know who you think you are. You came in my house. You will die today." We could hear Mr. Graves's feet as he was returning, running back up the stairs. Todd was still trying to get his duffel bag and his things, not moving fast enough for me and Rosie. Then we all heard Mr. Graves cocking his rifle as he was reaching the top of the stairs. That was when Todd understood he was safer in Vietnam than he was standing in our bedroom that day.

Todd jumped headfirst through the window. Then we threw his duffel bag out the window behind him. We could hear it hit the roof, just like we heard Todd hit the roof. It was too dark to see Todd, but we could hear all the tree branches breaking as he was grabbing and sliding down the tree. By the time his feet hit the ground, Mr. Graves took aim, trying his best to see Todd, and fired off his first shot. *Bam, boom,* the dogs were barking. We could hear the fence shaking as Todd was leaping over it. Mr. Graves leaned out the window and continued to fire shots up the alley until he ran out of bullets. Mr. Graves was firing mad. In all the times I had seen him angry, I had never seen him like this. He looked at me and Rosie and called us some kind of names, like nasty whores. Whore was the same name Shirley Pittman called my mother when I stuck that fork in her face. It hurt me so bad to hear him call us those names. There was no reasoning with him or talking to him. He was beyond all rationalization. He said he wanted us out of his house right now, and he was calling the police to have us removed. He told Mrs. Graves to have us get dressed before the police came. Mrs. Graves did as she was instructed. She told us we had really messed up now, and there was nothing she could do to help us, then she walked out the room. Rosie and I were still in shock and disbelief about the police. We both hopped back in our bunk beds and pulled the cover over our heads like that was going to make everything better or go away. I was mentally preparing myself for a bad whipping, but nothing could prepare me for what was getting ready to happen.

We could hear Mr. Graves's voice say, "Go on upstairs and get them there in the room at the far end of the hall." There was a firm knock on our bedroom door. Rosie and I both ignored the knock. Then a voice spoke out, insisting that we opened the door. They identified themselves as the police and repeated it, "This is the police, open the door." Rosie got up, and then I got up, and we slowly opened the door. To my disbelief, there were two tall, husky white men dressed in full police uniform, guns and all. They were standing at our bedroom door, saying, "Girls, you are going to have to change your pajamas and put some clothes and shoes on because you are going with us to juvenile hall." Stunned and still in disbelief, Rosie and I dropped our heads. The officer said, "We will stand outside the door while you girls change your clothes." Rosie and I changed our clothes. We opened the door, and the officers escorted us through the hall and downstairs. As we passed Mrs. Graves and Mr. Graves, they looked upon us with shame, not knowing that we were only trying to help a person in need by showing charity, what we were just taught in church earlier that day.

CHAPTER 47

. . . .

Juvenile Hall

The officers put us in the back of the police car. As they drove us to juvenile hall, one of the officers asked what we did. I was more than happy to tell him what we did. I said it was an act of kindness called charity we learned about in church earlier that day. The officer looked shocked to hear that. He just turned around and looked at his partner. They never said another word to us until we arrived at the back entrance of the juvenile hall. Once the police car came to a complete stop, one of the officers said, "I am sorry to hear you girls got in trouble trying to do something good. Now you are getting ready to enter a place where you must stay out of trouble and follow the rules. Other than that, things could get a lot worse for you." Then he said, "I wish you girls the best. You seem like well-mannered girls. Unfortunately, you now have to get processed into the detention center." He said, "There is a lady waiting for you girls right now." As we entered the facility from the back of the building, there was a lady standing at the back entrance waiting on us, just like the officer said. She had a big ring of keys in her hand. One of the officers looked sad and held his head down. As we walked toward the lady, the other officer said, "Well, it looks like our job is done here. So let me introduce you girls to Mrs. Locket. She will take it from here."

Mrs. Locket was a white lady about six feet tall, heavyset with short brown hair. She had a stern look on her face. You could tell she was not to be played with. She was standing there with all those keys in her hand. She definitely had the right name. Mrs. Locket said, "The first thing we are going to do is get you booked into our system. Then I have to confiscate all of your personal belongings. That includes all earrings, watches, and rings that you are wearing. And when you are released, your items will be returned to you." She asked what size the shoes and clothes we wore. She opened a closet and pulled out some clothes and shoes for me and Rosie and put them on the counter with the paperwork. "Now for the hard part," she said with a smirk on her face. "I am going to need you girls to strip all the way down, including your underwear." Then she handed us our uniforms and shoes. Mrs. Locket said, "As soon as I am finished processing you into the system, I will take you to the shower room. You can change your clothes there."

Once we were showered and dressed in those ugly uniforms, we were escorted to our cell. Since it was so late at night, there was only one other warden working that shift. It was eerily quiet. The only sound we could hear was, all those keys rattling as we walked Rosie to her cell. It was hard looking at Rosie walking into her cell and even harder watching the warden shut the door behind her. Then it was time for me to go to my cell. I was scared to death. Mrs. Locket said my cell was on the upper floor with my age group. We continued walking as she escorted me to my cell. Once we arrived, she quickly found the key on that big key ring and unlocked the door. The first thing I saw was a light shining through a small window on the wall directly in front of me. As my eyes scanned the room, I saw someone in the bottom bunk bed sleeping. Mrs. Locket said, "The top bunk is yours. As you can see, someone is already in the bottom bunk." She went on to say, "You're expected to get along with your cellmate and keep your room clean, and there is absolutely no talking or making any kind of sounds once the lights go out. And as you can see, the lights are already out, so the best thing you can do is go to sleep."

My roommate was sleeping so hard. She did not even wake up to see who was coming in her cell. As I lay in the bed looking at the light shining through the window, I got so afraid I started shaking. First of all, I was scared that I would fall off the top bunk. Second, I was terrified of being locked in a room with a total stranger. And third, Rosie could not help me in this situation. I began thinking how in the world we got ourselves in this mess. I concluded that we misinterpreted the Bible. I laid my head on the small pillow and covered myself with the blanket. I was trying not to make a sound and go to sleep. But the more I lay there, the more I thought about how we were attempting to do something good. How could it turn into something so bad? I began crying until my cries got loud and then louder. The sound was loud enough for the warden to hear me. She came to my cell and said if I did not shut it up, she would put me in solitary confinement. So I sucked it up and got quiet. I shut my mouth, then covered my mouth with my hands, trying not to make a sound. I let the tears run down the side of my face as I cried until I fell asleep.

The next day, I awoke to the sound of a buzzer. My cellmate was a Hispanic girl. She looked to be my age, and she did not speak English. She looked like she was more afraid of me than I was of her. That was a relief, considering that I had heard that a lot of bad things happened in juvenile hall. I had heard it was just like going to jail. There was a different warden that unlocked our door. I guessed the night shift warden was off work. The new warden told us to step out of our cell and form a single line in front of our cell. Once we stepped out of our cell, I could see the other girls lined up standing outside of their cells. They were in the front and back of us. We all formed one line, facing in the direction of the warden. The warden was standing at the front of the line. Suddenly, she yelled out, "No talking, stay close together in a single line, and follow me to the eating area." The eating area was a large room with lots of benches and tables. There were servers who put our food on our trays as we walked in front of them in a single line. The food was not too bad. I had eggs, toast, and oatmeal. I was so hungry anything would have tasted good at that time. After breakfast, we were given our assignments for that day. Another name for assignments was chores. Some girls' chores consisted of laundry duty, kitchen duty, or general cleaning duty. Cleaning could consist of doing dishes, mopping, washing walls, or helping fold and wash laundry, etc. There were boys that also stayed in juvenile hall, and occasionally, we would see them walking in line on an upper floor when they were being led to go to the cafeteria. They dared not to yell or attempt to speak to any one of us girls. They would just smile, wink, or try to wave.

One day, I was on my way to do laundry duty when I saw Rosie. She was in line following her group behind their warden. I was so excited when she saw me. She gave a big smile and waved her hand. I waved back and went to yell out, "Rosie, how are you doing?" She saw that I opened my mouth and prepared to yell. She lifted her hand to her mouth and put her finger to her lips, giving me a sign not to speak because she knew if I yelled out her name, it would have just gotten me into trouble. So I just watched her as she walked by in a single file. Tears started running down my face as my steps got slower and slower until the warden noticed me falling behind and getting out of line. She called out to me, "Hey, you, slowpoke, get back in line and keep up with the group." I did as I was told and wiped the tears from my eyes and stopped making whimpering sounds. I felt so isolated from society and family. I was trying to do my best, as an eleven-year-old, not to be afraid and obey all the different commands that were constantly given. I started becoming an introvert, not wanting to communicate with others. All I wanted to do was eat, sleep, and stay in my cell. Rosie and I managed to stay out of trouble by working hard, obeying all the rules, and keeping to ourselves.

Finally, the cavalry came, better known as my grandmother. The warden came to my cell and said I had a visitor. She said, "Her name is Mrs. Clark, so you need to follow me to the visitor area." I had never had a visitor before. I said to myself, "Mrs. Clark is my social worker. Maybe she is here to help get us out of this place." I was taken to a small room where Rosie and Mrs. Clark were already seated at a table. I ran over to Rosie and hugged her. Then I sat down next to her. The first thing that came out of Mrs. Clark's mouth was that she was so sorry. She said she had no idea that we were in juvenile hall until our grandmother called her. She said my grandmother found out when she called Mr. and Mrs. Graves. "She was just inquiring about your well-being in the foster home when they told her you girls had been gone for a few months. That is how we found out you girls were in juvenile hall." Mrs. Clark said, "I am sorry, but you girls had fallen through the cracks of the system." She continued to say she had no idea that we had been taken to juvenile hall, and she definitely would not have allowed us to be subjected to such an injustice. She said, "But not to worry, I am getting you out of here right now. I have made the necessary phone calls and filled out all the necessary paperwork to get you released immediately." I felt like one of the Hebrew children being freed from Pharaoh, as it was in the movie called *The Ten Commandments*.

CHAPTER 48

. . . .

Round Two with the Graves

Mrs. Clark did as she said and got us released. The only problem was, she was placing us back in the home with Mr. and Mrs. Graves. I was very hesitant about returning with the Graves. Mrs. Clark said she could not find another foster home that would take two girls our age. "I would have had to split you up," she said. "This was a short notice, and Mr. and Mrs. Graves agreed to take you back. Until I can find you a more suitable couple, you have no choice." Rosie and I were not mad at Mrs. Clark; we were disappointed in the Graves. I was hoping Mr. Graves and Mrs. Graves had gotten over their anger since the last time we had seen them. Mrs. Clark said they were willing to give us another chance, and hopefully, we could work things out with them. She drove us to the house and parked in front of it. She said there was no need for her to come inside this time, but if we needed her, we had her phone number. She was just a phone call away.

Rosie and I walked up to the door and knocked. Mrs. Graves came to the door and said, "Welcome back, girls."

Mr. Graves walked to the front door and said, "Hello, girls. Everything is still just like you left it in your room. You girls can go on back upstairs and get comfortable."

They never apologized. I was having a real hard time being around them both. I had lost respect for Mrs. Graves because she did not stand up for us, and I was in fear of being terrorized by Mr. Graves at any moment. That was what motivated me to figure out how to use the magic scarf by myself. Rosie was already in a bad mood most of the time before we went to juvenile hall. Now she was just downright angry every day. I tried to play the old maid game and Monopoly with Rosie, but it was like our innocence was stolen from us. Candy Land and Monopoly seemed like games for kids, and I did not feel like a kid anymore. I went and looked for my friend Duddy. When I found her, she was very attentive to every word I told her. She never questioned me or blamed me for what had happened. That was the first time Duddy told me she was going to pray for me. She tried to teach me more about her Catholic faith, but my mind was in a whole other place.

I decided to go visit my mom. I heard she had been doing well and managed to stay out of the hospital. What I did not know and much to my surprise, I was told my mom had given birth to a baby boy. I could hardly wait to set my eyes on this golden child. My mother had finally had the baby boy that she wanted for so many years. I made my way to her house the very next day. I found my mother happy and full of joy, sitting on the couch with a beautiful baby boy in her arms. Her boyfriend, Lubert, was sitting right there next to her. My mom said, "Look, Lane, come close and meet your baby brother. His name is Mark Tony Simpson." Momma was so happy she was glowing, and I was happy for her. I wanted to share with her what I had just been through at juvenile hall, but again, she was in her own world. She was busy sharing her joy and the love of her life with me. So as usual, I kept my problems to myself, not sharing one thing about juvenile hall. She did not even know we had been in juvenile hall.

My brother was a beautiful child. He weighed about seven pounds at birth and had light-brown eyes with curly black hair. The baby did not cry while I was there. He seemed to be a happy child. Lubert looked on, telling my mom to let me hold the baby. I could see the pride all over Lubert's face. It was his first child, and his parents' first and only grandchild. I finally felt like I could stop worrying about my mother. I felt like Lubert was doing a good job, and he could take care of her from here. As usual, at the end of my visit, I gave my hugs and kisses, and they gave me their well wishes and hugs.

On my way home, I started thinking about how happy my mom and Lubert looked. That started me to thinking about having my own family. All kinds of thoughts were running through my mind.

CHAPTER 49

. . . .

My Boyfriend Deno

Finally, I was almost home, and all I had to do was cross the street, and I would be on my block. While standing at the curb waiting for traffic to clear, I noticed a two-story redbrick apartment building with three guys sitting on the porch. They were listening to music and talking. One was tall, dark, and handsome, and the other two were short and had brown skin with no distinguishing features. I could not stop staring at the tall, dark young man. He noticed me looking and yelled out to me, saying, "Hey, good looking." Of course, I blushed and smiled. He waved, and I waved back. Then the traffic cleared enough for me to continue to cross the street. As I stepped off the curb, he yelled out, "Hold on, little lady, please wait a minute." I stopped in my tracks as he hopped of the porch and began running up to me. I thought it was really cool that I was being noticed by a guy, so I waited for him and did not cross the street. As he approached me, he yelled out, "Thank you for waiting." He asked me my name and told me his. He said his name was Deno. I had never heard a name like Deno before, and I had never seen a good-looking guy like this before. Deno was about six feet tall and dark as night. His hair was jet-black and shiny. I think he had one of those hairdos called a processed, like the singer James Brown had. His eyes were jet-black, and he had that perfect set of snow-white teeth.

I took one long look at him and thought, *This may be my future husband.* He asked me if he could walk with me. I explained I was going home. My house was just across the street, only a couple of houses from the corner. I continued to say my foster father did not allow us to bring boys to our house. Deno said, "No problem. I was just going to ask if you would like to walk with me to the doughnut shop on York Street." I thought about it briefly, then agreed, saying I would go. Having just left my mother's house and seeing my baby brother put me in a good mood. Plus, I was still thinking about having my own family. We turned and walked up Thirty-Second Street to avoid from walking directly in front of my house, hoping that Mrs. Graves or Mr. Graves would not see me walking with Deno. Deno showed himself to be a true gentleman. He did exactly as he said he would and walked me to the doughnut shop. He told me to pick out any donut I wanted; plus, he bought me a milkshake. We sat in the doughnut shop and talked and ate doughnuts for about an hour. I was used to sneaking out the window going to parties, but I never had a boyfriend to take me somewhere and buy me something. Deno told me he was in the process of buying a car, and he was looking for a nice girl like me to take different places. I asked him what kind of places. He replied places like the drive-in movies and restaurants that were not in walking distance. I agreed. I would be more than happy to accompany him when he got his car. Then he walked me back home the same way we went.

When we got back in front of his friend's apartment building, his two friends were still sitting on the front porch. He called over to the guys and said he wanted to introduce them to me. He was letting them know that he wanted me to be his girl so they would not try to talk to me. Then Deno walked me to the corner and watched me cross the street to ensure my safety. I was so happy I found myself skipping up the stairs on to the porch. I went straight to my bedroom, grabbed my little pink portable record player, and started playing some of my favorite forty-five records. I came across a record named "Just One Look" by Doris Troy. The song went, "Just one look, that is all it took." At that moment, it was like the song was speaking just to me. After listening to it over and over again, I said to myself, "I think I am falling in love, at least puppy love." I could not get Deno off my mind no matter what I did. A day or two passed and I could hardly wait to see him again.

It seemed as though all my sisters and I had suddenly met the man of our dreams. My sisters Rosie and Raney were dating brothers. Rosie was dating the younger brother named George. Raney was dating the brother named AC, who was a year older than George. The brothers had just moved to Denver from Battle Creek, Michigan, and were currently living with their sister Gladys on Twenty-Ninth and York Street. It was right down from the doughnut shop that Deno and I went to. Rosie said she really liked George. She said it felt a little odd that they were dating two brothers. I told Rosie I wanted to go with her the next time they went to meet the brothers. She said she would let me know as soon as they know the best day to go. Raney moved into a new foster home. It was only about eight blocks from our house. Raney's foster parents' names were Mr. and Mrs. Williams. Raney complained a lot about Mrs. Williams being too strict. Raney was considering moving in with AC since she was nearing the age that she could leave the foster care system. A week had passed, and I had not seen Deno, but I did get a chance to meet AC and George. They seemed to be genuinely nice and hospitable.

After a week, Deno showed up, just like he said, except this time, he was driving in front of my house in a new car. He waved at me to come across the street and to meet him in front of his friend's apartment. Once I reached him, I could see the big smile on his face. He said, "Look at my new car. I told you I was going to get one. It's a Ford, and it has a radio." He opened the car door for me and said, "This seat is reserved just for you." I felt like I was going to pass out. I was so excited. His friends were looking on with envy in their eyes. The first place he took me to was down on the Five Points. The Five Points was known for its nightlife and great soul food. Deno said he had a taste for a hot link. He described it as a big red spicy hot dog served on a bun with a side of fries. It sounded good to me. Plus, I was all about trying new things. While our food was being prepared, Deno asked me if it was okay if we went to City Park to eat our food. I answered, "Sure." That sounded really romantic. City Park was located about fifteen minutes away. When we arrived at the park,

Deno got a blanket out of the trunk of his car and spread it on the ground. He said he always wanted to have a picnic in the park with his favorite girl. We sat there and ate our hot links, fries, and pop and talked and laughed, just enjoying each other's company. After taking in the beautiful view of the blue sky with the mountains in the background and the smell of the green grass, it was more than I had hoped for.

A few more hours passed, and Deno said he better be getting me back home before it got dark. "But before we go, can I get a kiss?" I said yes, and he leaned over and gave me a peck on the lips. He was a perfect gentleman. Then we gathered up the blanket, and we drove back to the house. Since we were still trying to keep our dating a secret, I got out of the car across the street from my house. And again, he watched me walk to my house. The next weekend, we went to the drive-in movie. That was when I experienced my first real kiss, but Deno was still a gentleman. I had to tell Mrs. Graves a lie that I had attended a birthday party, and I lost track of time. She did not question my birthday story. And Mr. Graves had been staying out late every weekend, so he was not home to make a fuss. Deno and I continued to go out to eat and to the park.

CHAPTER 50

. . . .

Mr. Graves the Perfectionist

Mr. Graves started returning to his old ways, fussing all the time. As time went on, he continued to show signs of anger more and more frequently. We had started getting whippings with the belt for no real reason at all. It just seemed like part of our normal life to get a whipping. We knew ever so often we were going to get a whipping regardless. One day, Mr. Graves came home in one of his moods. He said, on his way in the house, he noticed some dog poop in the yard. He asked me and Rosie when was the last time we raked the lawn. The upkeep of the yard was one of Rosie's and my daily chores. We replied, "Yes, sir, we raked the yard yesterday."

He said, "Well, I am going to take a look at the backyard, and you girls better hope everything is in order back there." We knew when he said "Everything better be in order" that we were going to get a whipping because Mr. Graves was a perfectionist, and nothing was ever good enough for him. Taking care of the yard consisted of cutting, raking, edging, and removing all leaves and dog poop, putting them in the incinerator located in the backyard by the alley and burning them. The incinerator was about four by six feet, a brick with a large opening at the top and a small opening at the bottom. I hated putting dog poop in the incinerator because it smelled so bad especially when it was burning. I could not bear the smell of burning poop. It would make me sick to my stomach. When Mr. Graves was in the backyard, he saw some dog poop that we missed. H yelled and swore and had a fit. He made us go in the backyard and stand over the dog poop and look at it. He asked us, "Do you see this stuff?" Then he made us lean our heads over it and smell it. He said, "If you can see it and smell it, why is it still here?" Then he told us to go in the house to the sitting room, where he liked to whip us. He got his belt and whipped us. At the end of our whipping, he told us to go back and finish picking up the dog poop and burn it. I could never get used to getting a whipping, but Rosie got where a whipping did not faze her. She would not cry no matter what he did or how long he beat her. She became very defiant. She would just stand there and take it, not saying a word or shedding a tear. When he got tired of whipping us, he would just send us to our room.

Meanwhile, I was looking forward to another date with Deno. He said he wanted to take me somewhere new for our next date. I planned to wear a dress, but I still had whip marks on my legs from the whipping. I had been putting coco butter on the whip marks, but it was taking too long for them to fade away. I would probably have to cover my legs and were a pantsuit. After a few more days passed. It was finally the weekend. Deno showed up as usual, looking good and smelling good. I was so comfortable sitting in the front seat with his arm around me. We went to a soul-food restaurant and had a wonderful time. Deno continued to be a perfect gentleman. It had gotten late, but I did not want the night to end. When Deno took me home, Mrs. Graves had already gone to bed, and Mr. Graves was still out for the night. That made my night complete, not having to get yelled at for coming home a little late and not having to make up a lie. Rosie was going over to her boyfriend's house more often, and I noticed she was taking more than her usual amount of liquor from Mr. Graves's bar. I thought she had started taking it over her boyfriend's house. I had decided to stop drinking liquor. Instead, I began listening to more music and a wider range of music.

CHAPTER 51

. . . .

Sometimes You Got to Cry

About two weeks later, Mr. Graves came home around eight o'clock at night. He was fussing about how he had found dust on the front-room table, and the front-room carpet had something on it. Anyway, he said it had not been vacuumed properly. Bottom line was, we were getting ready to get another whipping. This time, Rosie was truly fed up with the whippings, and when Mr. Graves called us to the sitting room as usual to get our whipping, Rosie refused come. So Mr. Graves got Mrs. Graves to bring Rosie downstairs to get her whipping. This infuriated Mr. Graves. He was so frustrated with trying to make Rosie cry when he whipped her, and now she was defying him by not coming down to get her whipping. He said, "I told you girls, if you're going to do something, do it right the first time, and we would not have to go through this." Then he grabbed me by the arm and started whipping me with his belt. I started hopping around, screaming and crying. I was trying to use my hand and arms to block some of the licks on my legs. He mostly whipped us on our hind legs and thighs.

When it was Rosie's turn to get her whipping, Rosie did not come toward Mr. Graves when he called her. She just stood there, as if he was not talking to her. He got so angry he walked over to her and yanked her by the arm. He just started hitting her as hard as he could with that belt. Rosie did not hop, jump, cry, or make a sound. She just stood there like a statue. He continued to beat her with the belt. She acted like she had no feeling in her body. Mr. Graves was so upset he was yelling and cursing at her, saying things like, "So you think you are so tough. You think you will not cry. Oh, I will make you cry, little heifer!" Rosie just looked at him with a stern look in her eye, like she hated him. That took him over the edge, and he turned Rosie's arm loose. He started unbuckling his belt buckle around his waist. He said, "I got something for you. I bet this will make you cry." When Mr. Graves unbuckled his belt, he yanked the belt from around his waist in one fast twirl. When he did that, his pants had no support around his waist, and his pants dropped down to his knees. He was standing there in his boxer shorts, looking at us with that belt in his hand.

Rosie bust out laughing hysterically in a loud voice while pointing at his legs. She was laughing so hard she was bent over, holding her stomach. She yelled out, "Look at your skinny legs! Those are the skinniest legs I've ever seen."

That was when Mr. Graves snapped. I think he lost his mind looking at Rosie mocking him. Mr. Graves said, "I have had enough of you, Rosie, and I am going to kill you."

Mrs. Graves knew when he said he was going to kill Rosie, he meant it. Rosie was still standing there smiling. Mr. Graves pulled his pants up and put his belt on, then ran to the closet where he kept his rifle. When I saw him running to the closet after saying he was going to kill Rosie, I yelled, "Rosie, run out the door and run for your life!" I did not think Rosie thought he was actually going to do it because she stood there while he went to the closet. Once he reached in the closet and yanked out his rifle, Rosie's life flashed before her eyes. Rosie had taken first place in track at school, and she was runner-up in the state track championship. This was the day her speed was going to save her life. When Mr. Graves pulled his rifle out of the closet, Rosie hit the door, running. Mr. Graves cocked his rifle and took aim at Rosie, trying his best to shoot her as she ran down the street. *Bang, bam, boom* were all you could here. It was a wonder Mr. Graves did not shoot or kill one of our neighbors or an innocent bystander accidentally. I was yelling, "Mr. Graves, please do not kill her! Please do not shoot Rosie! Please stop, Mr. Graves, please!" I was crying on my knees at his feet, holding on to his pants' legs.

Mrs. Graves yelled out, "Roy, stop! You are going to kill her! Stop!"

Mr. Graves continued shooting until Rosie was out of his sight or he ran out of bullets. As soon as he stopped shooting, I ran out the door after Rosie. There were three things going on in my mind. One, I did not want to be in the house with Mr. Graves and his rifle. Two, I wanted to make sure Rosie had not gotten hit with a bullet. Three, I just did not know what else to do. I went running down the street after Rosie, yelling out her name. As I got far enough away from the house, I started trying to figure out where she might go. Then I thought she might have gone to her boyfriend's house. So I turned and went in that direction, checking along the ground to see if there was a trail of blood droppings. I needed to know if she had been shot, and the blood would help me track her direction. I did not find any blood to indicate that she had been shot.

Once I reached George's house, I knocked on the door, and his sister Gladys answered and said, "You must be looking for Rosie. Come on in." Rosie was sitting on the couch crying, and George was comforting her.

I ran over to her and hugged her, asking her, "Why didn't you just cry? He almost killed you."

She replied in a soft voice, "I know, Lane, I know," with tears running down her face. That was one of the few times I'd seen Rosie cry. I stayed there overnight with her and George's family.

When I awoke, I told Rosie I was going back home to see if Mr. Graves had settled down and would allow her to come back home. Rosie did not really want to come back home, but her boyfriend did not have a job, and he was living with his sister Gladys. Rosie had not turned sixteen years old yet, so she was too young to get a job and was still property of the state of Colorado. I told Rosie I was going to call our social worker and tell her everything that happened. I also told Rosie I did not feel safe in the house without her. I said he would probably kill me too if I was by myself. I did not really believe that, but I was hoping it would help encourage Rosie to come back home.

I called our social worker, Mrs. Clark, and told her everything that happened. Mrs. Clark said she had already spoken to Mrs. Graves, and it was okay for Rosie to return.

CHAPTER 52

. . . .

The Betrayal

When I got home, Mrs. Graves was apologetic, saying Mr. Graves had no business shooting his rifle at Rosie and she wanted Rosie to come back home. Mr. Graves agreed to her coming back at least until another suitable foster home was available. I returned to tell Rosie what Mrs. Grave said. Rosie did not want to come back home. I talked to her and reminded her about the situation she was in, that she was still property of the state of Colorado. And her choices were to come back to the Graves, go to another foster home, or go back to juvenile hall. She said, "When you put it that way, I guess I do not have any other choice but to go back." Rosie and I walked back to the house. When we entered into the house, Mrs. Graves was very apologetic to Rosie. Mr. Graves had no apology, but he didn't display any anger either. Once we were settled back in the house, we all tried to act like a normal family, but you could cut the air with a knife for the first couple of weeks. Then things seemed to mellow out, and Mr. Graves was not fussing, and we were not getting any more whippings. It seemed like maybe things were going to change.

Then our social worker, Mrs. Clark, called and said she was coming by the house to speak with me and Rosie about going on a camping trip. "That sounds great," Rosie and I replied. It would give us a chance to get away from everything and have a change of atmosphere. Mr. Graves and Mrs. Graves seemed pretty happy with the idea of me and Rosie going out of town. It was supposed to be for a week at an all-girls campground. Our social worker did not give us a whole lot of details. She just said we would learn more when we got closer to our travel date, which was two weeks away. Mrs. Graves bought us a lot of extra stuff for the trip. She even brought us two big metal suitcases. We looked like we were going away for a month or more the way Mrs. Graves was helping us pack. The day had come to get loaded up in the car and head to the campgrounds. Rosie and I were trying to inform all our friends we would be gone for a week, but I was unable to reach Deno. I did not know how to reach him. He did not have a phone. I figured he would be all right missing me for a week. Rosie informed all her friends and her boyfriend, George. We also let our sister Raney and my friend Duddy know how long we would be gone.

When it was time to go, Mrs. Graves was extremely nice. She was helping us load our things in the car. We said our goodbyes and was off for a week of fun. After a few hours of riding and passing through Colorado Springs, Rosie and I both started to wonder where this campground was. We asked Mrs. Clark, "Could you tell us a little bit more about the camp's location?"

She said, "It is in a small town that you would not know even if I told you. It is only another hour's drive, so be patient."

Rosie and I both complained, saying, "What another hour's drive?" We knew from going to Pueblo with our granny and taking fishing trips that this was an unusually long drive. We had never heard of any camps for children this far away from Denver, so Rosie and I inquired again, "Are there going to be a lot of children? What is the name of the camp? Why is it so far out?"

Mrs. Clark yelled, "If you girls do not stop asking me all these questions, you will see for yourself in just a little bit."

So Rosie and I trusted her and did not ask any more questions. When Rosie and I saw the sign saying "You are now entering Pueblo," we brought it to her attention what the sign said. Then we asked if the camp was in Pueblo. She replied, "Yes, you figured it out. It is in Pueblo, and we'll be pulling up in just a few moments." She pulled off the highway and into a neighborhood. She continued to drive several blocks, passing small, one-story brick homes. Then she pulled up to a big, two-story brick house, big enough to be a small business. Rosie and I looked at each other and said, "What! This does not look like a camp. What kind of building is this?" We asked, "And who lives here? Are we picking up some children from here or what?"

Instead of answering our questions, Mrs. Clark started crying and looking really pitiful. She had a look of shame on her face. Rosie and I were wondering what was going on. Then Mrs. Clark said something very shocking that we did not see coming. She said, "This is your new home. I did not have the heart to tell you. I could not find you another foster home in Denver that would keep you girls together." She said, "Most foster parents prefer younger children under the age of ten, and this was the only place that would take both you and your sister in." She continued to elaborate, saying because Rosie and I had reached twelve and thirteen years of age that she had no other options if she was going to keep us together.

I asked Mrs. Clark (in an angry voice) why she misled us into thinking we were going to an all-girls camp for a few weeks? Why not just tell us the truth? She said she just did not have the heart or strength to tell us the truth. She said after Rosie and I went to juvenile hall, our lives were like one big fire, constantly in one turmoil or another and, considering all that we had endured and tried so hard to overcome, that life just was not fair to us. She said having the responsibility and burden to tell us the truth that we had to move to an orphanage in another city and leave our schools, friends, and family behind was more than she could bear. So she said it was just easier to make up a lie. She started crying again, saying, "Girls, I am so sorry, please forgive me." Rosie and I felt so betrayed by the one person that we finally began to trust. We asked Mrs. Clark how she could do this to us when we trusted her. How could she lie like that on our ride all the way up here? She just broke down crying, saying, "I am so sorry, girls, I am so sorry." Then she looked up and saw a couple of ladies standing at the front door waving their hands, signaling for us to come up to the door. She said, "That is your new home, and they are your new caretakers. And it is now time for you girls to go meet them."

At this point, Rosie and I were so hurt, angry, and disappointed we could not speak. I said to myself that this was so wrong, but there was nothing we could do. We were still property of the state of Colorado, and if they said we had to stay in Pueblo at an orphanage, we had to stay there. So Rosie and I picked up our bags and suitcases, took them out of the car, and placed them on the sidewalk. We were standing there dejected, waiting for Mrs. Clark to get out of the car and walk us to the door to introduce us to our new caretakers. Instead, she said she did not have the strength to get out of the car and continued to cry, asking if we had all our things out of the car. When we replied yes, she drove off without looking back or even saying goodbye. Rosie and I picked up our things and walked up to the door. The two Black ladies were standing in the door with their arms stretched out, ready to greet us. They both said, "Girls, welcome to Lincoln Home orphanage for colored children. This is your new home."

To Be Continued

ABOUT THE AUTHOR

. . . .

Elaine was born in the beautiful Mile High City of Denver, Colorado. She has two wonderful children and two lovely grandchildren. As a child, Elaine often felt a strong desire to become an accomplished artist. She also desired to become a professional comedian. Elaine found peace and joy in telling a good joke. Painting a picture was like going to therapy. It was so relaxing. Elaine continued with her passion as an artist in between jobs, making sure to keep a positive attitude wherever she went. Elaine moved to East St. Louis, Illinois, and obtained her GED. Elaine also attended the local State Community College seeking a degree in business administration. She immediately began working for the University of Illinois cooperative extension service for seven years. Elaine later moved to Jennings, Missouri. There she was employed by Emerson Electric space and electronics division for six years. Elaine moved one more time to Huntsville, Alabama, where she has resided with her family for the past twenty-five years. Elaine was employed by Nissan auto sales for five years, then she returned back to work in the electrical field. She was employed by several electric companies, starting with Benchmark Electronics, ADTRAN Electronics, and Tyonek Electronics. When the pandemic hit in 2020, Elaine could no longer work at Tyonek. She said, "Now is the time to write my book and tell my story." And just like that, she began writing, and her first novel was born. Elaine has exhibited her paintings at galleries, on TV, and in newspapers. She received a culture showcase award from Boeing and an officially commended award from Department of the Army.

CPSIA information can be obtained
at www.ICGtesting.com
Printed in the USA
BVHW031532050122
625453BV00004B/276